AN INTRODUCTION TO

THE SCIENCES OF THE QUR'AN

AN INTRODUCTION TO

THE SCIENCES OF THE QUR'AN

BY **FURHAN ZUBAIRI**

Printed in the United States of America

First Publishing, 2017

ISBN-13: 978-1548698577
ISBN-10: 1548698571

Cover design, layout, and typesetting: Mohammad Bibi
Typeset in Lato, Nassim and Ubuntu

Dedicated to my parents, family and teachers.
May Allah continue to bless them and grant them
the highest ranks in Paradise.

CONTENTS

INTRODUCTION XVII

CHAPTER 1 'ULUM AL-QUR'AN
Definition 1
Subject Matter 1
Purpose 2
Objective 2

CHAPTER 2 AL-QUR'AN
Linguistic 4
Technical 4

CHAPTER 3 WAHY
Definition 7
Types of Waḥy 7
How Waḥy came to the Prophet ﷺ 8
Stages of Revelation 10
First and Last Revelation 11

CHAPTER 4 PRESERVATION & COMPILATION
The Era of the Prophet ﷺ 13
The Era of Abū Bakr رضي الله عنه 16
The Era of 'Uthmān رضي الله عنه 18

CHAPTER 5 SUBJECT MATTER
Beliefs 22
Commandments 23
Stories 24
Parables 25

CHAPTER 6
MAKKI & MADANI

What is meant by Makki and Madani? 27
How is it known if a verse or surah is Makki or Madani? 28
Themes of Makki and Madani Revelation 28
Characteristics of Makki and Madani Revelation 30
How Verses and Surahs are Classified as Makki or Madani 30
Importance 31

CHAPTER 7
CAUSES OF REVELATION

Examples 33
Importance 34
Is consideration given to the words' general meanings or the specific cause? 35

CHAPTER 8
ABROGATION

Definition 37
Proof of Abrogation 38
Examples 38
Types of Abrogation 39
Importance 41

CHAPTER 9
THE SEVEN LETTERS & DIFFERENT RECITATIONS

The Seven Letters 43
A Few Narrations Regarding the Seven Letters 44
What are the Seven Letters? 45
The Different Recitations 45

CHAPTER 10
TAFSIR

Definition 47
Importance 48
Sources of Tafsīr 49
Tafsīr of Qur'ān by Qur'ān 50
Tafsīr of Qur'ān by Sunnah 51
Tafsīr of Qur'ān by the Narrations of Companions ﷺ 52
Tafsīr of Qur'ān by the Narrations of Successors 53
Tafsīr of Qur'ān through the Arabic Language 54
Tafsīr of Qur'ān through Personal Interpretation 55
Famous Works of Tafsīr 56

CHAPTER 11
HOW TO APPROACH THE QUR'AN

Structure of the Qur'ān 62
Studying the Qur'ān 63

FURTHER READING 65
BIBLIOGRAPHY 67
NOTES 73

Transliteration & Pronunciation Key

Arabic Letter	Transliteration	Sound
ء	ʾ	A slight catch in the breath, cutting slightly short the preceding syllable.
ا	*ā*	An elongated *a* as in *cat.*
ب	*b*	As in *best.*
ت	*t*	As in *ten.*
ث	*th*	As in *thin.*
ج	*j*	As in *jewel.*
ح	*ḥ*	Tensely breathed *h* sound made by dropping tongue into back of throat, forcing the air out.
خ	*kh*	Pronounced like the *ch* in Scottish *loch*, made by touching back of tongue to roof of mouth and forcing air out.
د	*d*	As in *depth.*
ذ	*dh*	A thicker *th* sound as in *the.*
ر	*r*	A rolled *r*, similar to Spanish.
ز	*z*	As in *zest.*
س	*s*	As in *seen.*
ش	*sh*	As in *sheer.*
ص	*ṣ*	A heavy *s* pronounced far back in the mouth with the mouth hollowed to produce full sound.
ض	*ḍ*	A heavy *d/dh* pronounced far back in the mouth with the mouth hollowed to produce a full sound.
ط	*ṭ*	A heavy *t* pronounced far back in the mouth with the mouth hollowed to produce a full sound.
ظ	*ẓ*	A heavy *dh* pronounced far back in the mouth with the mouth hollowed to produce a full sound.
ع	ʿ	A guttural sound pronouned narrowing the throat.
غ	*gh*	Pronounced like a throaty French *r* with the mouth hallowed.
ف	*f*	As in *feel.*
ق	*q*	A guttural *q* sound made from the back of the throat with the mouth hallowed.
ك	*k*	As in *kit.*
ل	*l*	As in *lip.*
م	*m*	As in *melt.*
ن	*n*	As in *nest.*
هـ	*h*	As in *hen.*

و	*w* (at the beg. of syllable)	As in *west*.
	ū (in the middle of syllable)	An elongated *oo* sound, as in *boo*.
ي	*y* (at beg. of syllable)	As in *yes*.
	ī (in the middle of syllable)	An elongated *ee* sound, as in *seen*.

ﷻ Used following the mention of Allah, God, translated as, "The Almighty."

ﷺ Used following the mention of the Prophet Muhammad, translated as, "May God honor and protect him."

عليه السلام Used following the mention of any other prophet or Gabriel, translated as, "May God's protection be upon him."

رضي الله عنهم Used following the mention of the Prophet Muhammad's companions, translated as, "May God be pleased with them."

رضي الله عنه Used following the mention of a male companion of the Prophet Muhammad, translated as, "May God be pleased with him."

رضي الله عنها Used following the mention of a female companion of the Prophet Muhammad, translated as, "May God be pleased with her."

رحمهم الله Used following the mention of the major scholars of Islam, translated as, "May God have mercy on them."

رحمه الله Used following the mention of a major scholar of Islam, translated as, "May God have mercy on him."

INTRODUCTION
FROM THE AUTHOR

In the name of Allāh the Most Merciful,
the Very Merciful.

All thanks and praise are due to Allāh ﷻ, the Lord of the worlds, and may His peace and blessings be upon His last and final messenger, Muḥammad ﷺ, his family, his companions, and those who follow them until the end of times.

Without a doubt the Qur'ān is the most important book in the life of a Muslim. That is because the Qur'ān is not simply a book; it is the divine speech of Allāh ﷻ -- His words revealed to the Prophet ﷺ. It is the last and final revelation sent for the guidance of humanity for all times and all places. It is the primary source of beliefs, rituals, ethics, morals, and laws in Islām. Our entire lives as Muslims revolve around the teachings of the Qur'ān.

Every single aspect of the Qur'ān is held to be sacred. Due to that, Muslims throughout the world, across diverse cultures, treat the Qur'ān with the highest level of respect, honor, and reverence. Each culture has its own unique ways and practices for showing its love and respect for the book of Allāh. Although these practices may not be rooted in the religion itself, they are done as a sign of honor. There are copies of the Qur'ān in every single household throughout the Muslim world. In these households, the Qur'ān is placed on the highest shelf or the most honored space. Beautiful, elaborate, and expensive covers are made for it. It is considered disrespectful for the Qur'ān to be placed on the floor or for one's feet to be pointed towards it. When it is recited people stop speaking and women who may not regularly do so will cover their hair. People wear verses of the Qur'ān around their necks for protection. The Qur'ān is considered to be a source of immense blessings. Basically, we as Muslims do many unique things to show our love and respect for the Qur'ān.

However, true love and respect for the Qur'ān is expressed through reading it, understanding its message, and applying it to our lives. We use it as a source of guidance to navigate through the world and live a life that is pleasing to Allāh ﷻ. It is literally our manual for life that we use to build a path towards the Divine. It is supposed to be our inspiration, encouragement, and tool we use to deal with the challenges of life. It contains guidance for every single aspect of our lives: theological, spiritual, individual, communal, economic, and political.

The primary objective of the Qur'ān is for us to think, ponder, and reflect over its meanings. As Allāh ﷻ tells us, "[This is] a blessed Book which We have revealed to you, [O Muḥammad], that they might reflect upon its verses and that those of understanding would be reminded."[1] However, in order to do so, we have to actually have an understanding of the Qur'ān and its message. We have to have an active and engaging relationship with the words of Allāh ﷻ. For the vast majority of us as Muslims living in America, as well as Muslims in different parts of the world, that can be very challenging.

It is difficult to do so for a number of different reasons. Most Muslims do not know the Arabic language and therefore have to rely on translations that cannot capture the eloquence, power, beauty, and miraculous nature of Allāh's divine words. When reading through a translation that is devoid of context, background, explanations, and commentary, it is hard to engage with the Qur'ān on a spiritual and intellectual level.

Another reason is that we as Muslims tend to have a rather shallow understanding of our own religion. For the most part, our knowledge of Islām is limited to what our parents taught us, what we learned for a few hours a week in Sunday school, as well as what we have heard from a few lectures here and there. So our understanding of Islām is limited and oftentimes tainted

---

1 Qur'ān 38:29

with culture. This shallow understanding of Islām has led to what some call a "crisis of knowledge."

This is perhaps the greatest crisis affecting the entire Muslim World. It is reflected in how Islām is taught, practiced, and understood. The only way to rescue ourselves from this crisis is through knowledge and having a structured methodology for studying our own religion. There is a common level of literacy regarding Islām that every Muslim should have. Part of that base level of literacy is having a proper understanding of what exactly the Qur'ān is: its history, preservation, compilation, subject matter, and themes. We need to have a proper framework and methodology for approaching a study of the Qur'ān.

Alḥamdulillāh, through the grace and mercy of Allāh, I have been blessed with the opportunity to develop and teach a course through IOK Extension on the Sciences of the Qur'ān. While preparing for the course, I compiled a set of personal notes that I would use to teach the class. Students would often ask me to send them a copy of the notes to use as a personal reference and a study guide. The course was also taught to the IOK Seminary students before they began their study of tafsīr. I thought that it would be beneficial for our students, as well as other students of knowledge, to compile my notes into a short booklet that can serve as a brief introduction to the Sciences of the Qur'ān to help establish a base level of literacy within the subject. The purpose of this booklet is to provide, what I consider, something similar to cliff notes for the Sciences of the Qur'ān.

I compiled the notes primarily from four sources: 1) *An Approach to the Quranic Sciences* by my esteemed teacher Mufti Taqi Usmani, 2) *An Introduction to the Sciences of the Qur'aan* by Dr. Yasir Qadhi, 3) *Al-Tibyān fī ʿUlūm Al-Qur'ān* by Shaykh Muḥammad ʿAli Al-Ṣābūni, and 4) *Al-Itqān fī ʿUlūm Al-Quran* by the eminent scholar and ascetic, Jalāl Al-Dīn Al-Suyūṭī ﵀.

I would like to thank all of those individuals who provided suggestions, comments, improvements and took the time out of their busy schedules to edit this short work. May Allah ﷻ reward our IOK Seminary student Sr. Ayesha Hussain and my good friend and old roommate Sh. Muneeb Baig, continue to bless them and increase them in knowledge.

I ask Allāh ﷻ to bless this small effort and make it beneficial for those who read it. I ask Allāh ﷻ to bless all of us with a strong relationship with the Qur'ān so that we can engage it, ponder over its meanings, and bring its blessing into our lives. May Allāh shower His blessings and mercy upon His last and final messenger, Muḥammad ﷺ.

Furhan Zubairi
Diamond Bar, CA
November 19, 2015 / Ṣafar 8, 1437

1

'ULUM AL-QUR'AN

THE SCIENCES OF THE QUR'AN

Before approaching the study of any discipline, it is part of the Islamic Scholarly tradition to first discuss a few preliminary remarks regarding that discipline. These preliminary remarks are called the mabādī, which are the definition, subject matter, purpose, and objective of the discipline itself. The mabādī allow a student to approach the subject with a very basic understanding of what is going to be studied.

DEFINITION

ʿUlūm al-Qurʾān is a compound structure made up of two words, ʿulūm and al-Qurʾān. ʿUlūm is the plural of ʿilm, which means knowledge, and in this context it means a science, discipline, study or branch of knowledge. Al-Qurʾān is the proper name for the final revelation of Allāh ﷻ sent for the guidance of mankind. A detailed definition of the word will be mentioned in the next chapter. The term is usually translated as the Sciences of the Qurʾān or Qurʾānic studies.

SUBJECT MATTER

The Sciences of the Qurʾān is an extremely vast field of Islamic scholarship that deals with the study of various aspects of the Qur'ān. It discusses the revelation, preservation, compilation, order, and arrangement of the text itself. It covers the subject matter of the Qur'ān, the causes of revelation, the classification of verses and chapters into Makkī and Madanī, the concept of abrogation, the miraculous nature of the Qur'ān, and other various discussions related to the Qur'ān. Basically, it is a branch of knowledge that gathers all of the various fields of study associated with any aspect of the Qur'ān.

PURPOSE

The purpose of studying the Sciences of the Qur'ān is to understand the final revelation of Allāh ﷻ properly in the light of how the Prophet ﷺ, his Companions, and their students understood it.

OBJECTIVE

The main objective behind studying any Islamic Science is to attain the pleasure of Allāh ﷻ in order to be successful in this life and the next.

2

AL-QUR'AN

In order to get a feeling for the greatness of the Qur'ān it is enough to say that it is the uncreated speech of Allāh ﷻ, the Creator of the Heavens and the Earth and everything they contain. It is the last and final revelation sent for the guidance of humanity until the end of times. Its words are so powerful, emotive, and effective that if they were to be revealed on a mountain, it would be humbled and burst apart out of the awe of Allāh[2]. Its recitation, memorization, interpretation, understanding, teaching, and learning are all acts of worship that bring blessings and reward. These words are a source of light, guidance, cure, and mercy.

Since the time of the Qur'ān's revelation until today, the Muslim community has served the Book of Allāh in numerous ways, leaving behind a very rich and exhaustive tradition. But none can ever claim to have done complete justice to the Book; it remains an ocean that calls devotees of every era to dive into its depths to extract new pearls and treasures. There are many descriptions of the Qur'ān written by great linguists and poets, but there is none more eloquent than the description of the Prophet ﷺ himself. The Prophet ﷺ said, "Allāh's book. In it is news of those before you, information about what comes after you, and judgment for what happens between you. It is the Criterion (between right and wrong) without jest. Whoever among

2 Qur'ān, 59:21

the oppressors abandons it, Allāh crushes him, and whoever seeks guidance from other than it, then Allāh leaves him to stray. It is the firm rope of Allāh, the wise remembrance, the straight path. It is the one that desires cannot distort, nor can the tongues twist, nor can the scholars ever have enough of it. It shall not become dull from repetition, and the wonders of it do not diminish. It is the one that when the Jinns heard it, they did not hesitate to say about it: 'Verily, we have heard a wonderful Recitation (this Qur'ān)! It guides to the Right Path, and we have believed therein.' Whoever speaks according to it has spoken the truth; whoever acts according to it is rewarded; whoever judges by it has been just, and whoever invites to it has been guided to the straight path."[3]

When talking about definitions, scholars talk about the linguistic as well as the technical meaning of a word. Words have linguistic definitions but often times because of coinage, usage, custom, and other factors, they take on different meanings.

LINGUISTIC

Linguistically, the word Qur'ān is derived from the root verb *qara'a* (قرأ) which means to read or to recite. So the word Qur'ān is the verbal noun, which means the reading or the recitation. The word Qur'ān literally means the reading, the recitation, or that which is read or recited. One of the reasons why it has been named the Qur'ān is because it is a book that is recited by Muslims throughout the world and will continue to be recited until the end of times.

TECHNICAL

Scholars are very precise when defining terms by using exact language and carefully choosing words. A good definition has to be both inclusive and exclusive; inclusive means that it has to include everything that is essential to the term being defined and exclusive means that it has to exclude everything that is extraneous to the term.

The agreed upon definition of the Qur'ān is that it is the inimitable Arabic speech of Allāh ﷻ that He revealed to Muḥammad ﷺ through the An-

3 al-Tirmidhī, *k. faḍā'il Al-Qur'ān 'an rasūl Allāh*, 3153

gel Jibrīl ﷺ, which has been preserved in the maṣāḥif (written copies of the Qur'ān), and has reached us by mutawātir transmission.

The **first** part of the definition, "the inimitable Arabic...," establishes two things: the miraculous nature of the Qur'ān and that the Qur'ān is in the Arabic language. Part of the miracle of the Qur'ān is that no one can produce anything similar to it. By mentioning that the Qur'ān is in Arabic, all translations of the text are excluded from the definition.

The **second** part of the definition states that the Qur'ān is the "speech of Allāh" This excludes the speech of any other creation, which includes the statements of the Prophet ﷺ. The Qur'ān is the speech of Allāh ﷻ that He spoke in a manner that is befitting to Him. That is why the ḥadīth are not considered to be Qur'ān.

The **third** part of the definition, "that He revealed to Muḥammad ﷺ" excludes revelation sent to the previous Prophets such as Mūsā and 'Īsā ﷺ.

The fourth part of the definition, "through the Angel Jibrīl ﷺ" limits the Qur'ān to revelation the Prophet ﷺ received through Jibrīl. There were other ways the Prophet ﷺ received revelation that will be mentioned in chapter three.

The **fifth** part of the definition, "which has been preserved in the maṣāḥif," refers to the copies of the Qur'ān that were written during the time of 'Uthmān ﷺ and distributed throughout the Muslim world. The significance of this will be mentioned in chapter four.

The **last** part of the definition, "and has reached us by mutawātir transmission," explains how the Qur'ān has reached us from the time of the Prophet ﷺ. A report is considered to be mutawātir when it is transmitted by a large number of people in each generation so that it is impossible for them to have agreed upon a lie either intentionally or unintentionally. Basically, so many people transmitted it that it is impossible for it to be a forgery. Something that is transmitted through tawātur gives the benefit of certainty.

This is the technical definition formulated by the scholars of uṣūl and fiqh. The purpose of this definition is to simply identify what is meant by the word "Qur'ān" and not to capture the actual essence of the Qur'ān. Beyond this definition, and perhaps more important, is to understand that the Qur'ān is a book of guidance. Everything that is mentioned in the Qur'ān is done so for the guidance of humanity. The stories and parables, commands and prohibitions, signs in the universe and the human body, and everything else mentioned is for guidance. Allāh ﷻ Himself describes the Qur'ān as "guidance for mankind."[4] It provides guidance for literally every single aspect of human life.

4 Qur'ān, 2:185

3

WAHY

REVELATION

Since the Prophet ﷺ received the Qur'ān through waḥy (revelation), it is important to understand the concept of waḥy and its different forms.

DEFINITION

Linguistically, waḥy is the verbal noun from the verb *waḥā* (وحى), which means to reveal or to inspire. So the word "waḥy" literally means revelation or inspiration.

Technically, waḥy refers to the speech of Allāh ﷻ revealed to one of His Prophets or Messengers. It is the way that Allāh ﷻ chose to communicate with His prophets and messengers. Some of the means of this transmission are described below.

TYPES OF WAHY

Regarding the forms of waḥy, Allāh ﷻ says, "And it is not for any human being that Allāh should speak to him except by revelation or from behind a partition or that He sends a messenger to reveal, by His permission, what He wills. Indeed, He is Most High and Wise."[5] Three kinds of waḥy are understood from this verse:

5 Qur'ān, 43:51

1. INSPIRATION DIRECTED INTO THE PROPHET'S HEART.

Allāh ﷻ inspires the message directly into the heart of a Prophet without the means of an intermediary. No one is seen and no voice is heard, but the message is placed directly into the heart of the Prophet. This type of waḥy can happen while the Prophet is awake or asleep.

2. DIRECT SPEECH OF ALLĀH ﷻ FROM BEHIND A VEIL.

Allāh ﷻ speaks directly to the Prophet from behind a veil. Allāh ﷻ is not seen however a voice is heard. This voice is something unique to Allāh ﷻ and does not resemble the voice of any creation but is recognized by the Prophet.

3. INSPIRATION THROUGH AN ANGEL.

Allāh ﷻ sends the message through the angel Jibrīl عليه السلام, who either conveys the message through voice only, comes in the form of a human being, or comes in his original form.

HOW WAHY CAME TO THE PROPHET ﷺ

The Prophet ﷺ received revelation in six different ways.

1. TRUE DREAMS

As a precursor to revelation, the Prophet ﷺ would see particular dreams and whatever he saw in those dreams would come true. ʿĀ'ishah رضي الله عنها narrated, "The commencement of divine revelation to Allāh's Messenger ﷺ was in the form of good dreams. He never used to dream about anything except that it came true like the rising of the sun."[6]

2. THE RINGING OF BELLS

ʿĀ'ishah رضي الله عنها narrated that al-Ḥārith ibn Hishām رضي الله عنه asked Allāh's Messenger ﷺ "O Allāh's Messenger! How does revelation come to you?" Allāh's Messenger ﷺ replied, "Sometimes it comes to me like the ringing of a bell. This form of revelation is the hardest of all and then this state passes off after I have grasped what is inspired."[7]

---

6 Bukhārī, *k. bad al- waḥy, b.*, 3

7 Bukhārī, *k. bad al- waḥy, b.*, 2

The Prophet ﷺ would sometimes hear a sound similar to the ringing of a bell; the sound of revelation would be continuous and would come from all directions. Some scholars mention the sound he heard was the voice of the Angel or the sound of its wings fluttering. This form of revelation was the most difficult upon the Prophet ﷺ. It is reported that when he received revelation through this form he would break into a severe sweat even on cold days.[8]

3. ANGEL COMING IN THE FORM OF A HUMAN

In the same narration of ʿĀ'ishah ﷺ mentioned above, the Prophet ﷺ said, "Sometimes the Angel comes in the form of a man and talks to me and I grasp whatever he says."[9]

The Angel Jibrīl would come to the Prophet ﷺ in the form of a human being. It is mentioned that sometimes he would take the shape of Ḍiḥyah al-Kalbī ﷺ, one of the companions of the Prophet ﷺ, and sometimes he would come as a stranger as is mentioned in the well-known hadith of 'Umar ﷺ.[10]

4. ANGEL COMING IN ITS ORIGINAL FORM

The Angel Jibrīl would bring revelation to the Prophet ﷺ in his original form. The Prophet ﷺ described him as having six-hundred wings and, in terms of size, filling the space between the heavens and earth.

This form of revelation was rare and only occurred a few times during Prophethood--once, when the Prophet ﷺ himself wanted to see Jibrīl in his original form, and another time during the journey of ascension to the heavens.

5. DIRECT SPEECH FROM ALLĀH ﷻ

Allāh ﷻ spoke directly to the Prophet ﷺ from behind a veil. This happened once during the ascension to the heavens. It is mentioned in a narration that Abū Dharr ﷺ asked the Prophet ﷺ, "Did you see your Lord?" He replied, "Light, how could I see Him?"[11] Some commentators mention that this ḥadīth means there was a veil of light between him and Allāh ﷻ.

---

8 Bukhārī, *k. bad al- waḥy, b.*, 2

9 Bukhārī, *k. bad al- waḥy, b.*, 2

10 Muslim, *k. Al-Imān, b. bayān al-īman wa al-islām wa al-ihsān*, 1

11 Muslim, *k. al-īmān, b. fī qawlihī 'alayhi al-salām nūr anna arāhu*, 350

6. INSPIRATION DIRECTED TO THE HEART

Jibrīl ﷺ would inspire something in the heart of the Prophet ﷺ without appearing in front of him. This method of revelation is derived from a few narrations. For example, the Prophet ﷺ said, "Jibrīl ﷺ inspired in my heart that none of you will leave this world until his sustenance has been made complete."

STAGES OF REVELATION

The Qur'ān is the eternal, uncreated speech of Allāh ﷻ. Speech is one of the attributes of Allāh ﷻ. Just as Allāh ﷻ is eternal and uncreated, similarly all of His attributes are eternal and uncreated. The theological discussion underlying this understanding is beyond the scope of this booklet, but it is important to know that this is part of traditional orthodox Muslim belief.

One of the first things that Allāh ﷻ created is the Pen, which was then commanded to write. Everything that is meant to happen in this world from the beginning of time until the end of time is written in the Preserved Tablet. The Qur'ān was also written in the Preserved Tablet. Allāh ﷻ tells us, "Rather it is the Glorious Qur'ān. In the Preserved Tablet."[12] From the Preserved Tablet, the Qur'ān was sent down in two stages.

In a narration, ʿAbdullah ibn ʿAbbās ؓ mentions both stages: "The entire Qur'ān was revealed to the lower heavens on the night of Power. Then whenever Allāh ﷻ wished to inspire something He would inspire it."[13]

STAGE ONE

The Qur'ān was revealed in its entirety from the Preserved Tablet to a place in the lower heavens known as the House of Honor. It is also known as Bayt al-Maʿmūr, or the Established House. It is a space in the lower heavens located directly above the Kaʿbah and is the place of worship of the angels. This revelation took place in the month of Ramadan on the night of Power.

When the Qur'ān refers to this initial revelation, it uses the verb derived from al-inzāl, which means to send down. Allāh ﷻ mentions the month in which this took place. "The month of Ramadan is the month in which the

12 Qur'ān, 85:21-22
13 Al-Mustadrak lil Hākim, 2878

Qur'ān was revealed."[14] Allāh ﷻ also mentions the night in which it was revealed: "Indeed, We sent it down on a blessed night."[15] In another verse, Allāh clarifies what He means by the blessed night when He says, "Indeed, We revealed it on the night of Power."[16] These verses are referring to the first stage of revelation.

STAGE TWO

The second stage was the gradual revelation of the Qur'ān to the Prophet ﷺ over a period of twenty-three years. During this time period, the Qur'ān was revealed bit by bit in response to specific circumstances, incidents, events, and questions. It started when the Prophet ﷺ was forty years old and continued until shortly before he left this world at the age of sixty-three. This revelation started in the month of Ramadan on the night of Power when Jibrīl ﷺ came to the Prophet ﷺ in the cave of Ḥirā.

FIRST AND LAST REVELATION

The first revelation sent to the Prophet ﷺ was the first five verses from Surah al-'Alaq. Ā'ishah ﷺ narrated, "The commencement of Divine revelation to Allāh's Messenger ﷺ was in the form of good dreams that came true like the breaking of day and then the love of seclusion was bestowed upon him. He used to go in seclusion in the cave of Hira where he used to worship (Allāh alone) continuously for many days before his desire to see his family. He used to take provisions for the stay and then come back to (his wife) Khadījah to take his food likewise again until suddenly the Truth descended upon him while he was in the cave of Hira. The angel came to him and asked him to read. The Prophet ﷺ replied, 'I do not know how to read.' The Prophet ﷺ added, 'The angel caught me (forcefully) and pressed me so hard that I could not bear it any more. He then released me and again asked me to read and I replied, 'I do not know how to read.' Thereupon he caught me again and pressed me a second time until I could not bear it any more. He then released me and again asked me to read but again I replied, 'I do not know how to read (or what shall I read)?' Thereupon he caught me for the third time and

14 Qur'ān, 2:185
15 Qur'ān, 44:3
16 Qur'ān, 97:1

pressed me, and then released me and said, 'Read in the name of your Lord, who has created (all that exists), created man from a clot. Read! And your Lord is the Most Generous.'[17] Then Allāh's Messenger ﷺ returned with the Inspiration and with his heart beating severely. Then he went to Khadījah bint Khuwaylid and said, 'Cover me! Cover me!' She covered him until his fear was over and after that he told her everything that had happened and said, 'I fear that something may happen to me.' Khadījah replied, 'Never! By Allāh, Allāh will never disgrace you. You keep good relations with your kith and kin, help the poor and the destitute, serve your guests generously and assist the deserving calamity-afflicted ones.'"[18]

After that there was a break in divine revelation for a period of three years, which is known as Fatrah al-Waḥy. Afterwards, Surah al-Muddathir was revealed.

The last verse to be revealed was verse 281 from Surah al-Baqarah. "And fear the day in which you will return to Allāh. Then everyone will be laid what they earned and they will not be dealt with unjustly."[19]

---

17 Qur'ān, 96:1-3

18 Bukhārī, *k. bad al-waḥy, b.*, 3

19 Qur'ān, 2: 28

4

PRESERVATION & COMPILATION

The Qur'ān is the only revealed scripture that has been guaranteed protection by Allāh. Allāh ﷻ Himself took the responsibility of preserving the Qur'ān. He says, "Indeed, it is We who sent down the Remembrance and indeed, We will be its guardian."[20] Allāh ﷻ has promised to protect the Qur'ān from any distortions, discrepancies, and additions or deletions. Through this divine protection, the words of the Qur'ān today are the exact same words that were revealed to the Prophet ﷺ. The care and attention to minute detail given in the preservation and compilation of the Qur'ān is unparalleled.

The preservation and compilation of the Qur'ān passed through three unique stages: the first was during the life of the Prophet ﷺ, the second was during the time of Abū Bakr رضي الله عنه, and the third was during the caliphate of 'Uthmān رضي الله عنه.

THE ERA OF THE PROPHET ﷺ

During the life of the Prophet ﷺ the Qur'ān was primarily preserved in two ways:

1. Orally through memorization
2. Writing

20 Qur'ān, 15:9

ORALLY

The primary method of preservation was memorization. The Arabs of the pre-Islamic era were mostly an illiterate nation. However it is important to understand that illiteracy does not mean non-intelligent. It simply refers to the fact that reading and writing were not common. Despite their inability to read and write, they were extremely eloquent and creative when it came to speech and poetry. What they lacked in terms of reading and writing was made up through their eloquence. They would have competitions in composing the most eloquent poems. Since the art of reading and writing was scarce and books were uncommon they were dependent on their memories for the preservation of these poems. As a matter of fact, because their access to writing and written materials was limited, their ability to memorize was enhanced. An average person would have thousands of lines of poetry memorized. Most people would have their own lineages memorized along with the lineages of their horses.

The Arabs had a very strong oral tradition of poetry and storytelling that enhanced their ability to memorize. It is no surprise that when revelation started coming to the Prophet ﷺ, his companions would commit those verses to their memories.

The Prophet ﷺ was the first to memorize the verses of the Qur'ān. Initially when he received revelation he would hastily repeat after Jibrīl عليه السلام to ensure that he would memorize the verses. Allāh ﷻ reassured him, "do not move your tongue with haste to recite it. It is for Us to collect it and give you the ability to recite it."[21] Allāh ﷻ assured the Prophet ﷺ that the words of the Qur'ān would be preserved in his heart as soon as they were revealed.

The Prophet ﷺ was constantly engaged in memorizing, teaching, recording, and explaining the Qur'ān. Not only did the Prophet ﷺ memorize the Qur'ān, but he also encouraged his companions to memorize and teach it as well. Through his words, he would offer incentives and encouragement for teaching and memorizing. For example, the Prophet ﷺ said, "The best amongst you are those who learn the Qur'ān and teach it."[22] In another statement the Prophet ﷺ said, "Whoever reads a letter from the book of Allāh, then for them is a good deed. A good deed is multiplied by ten. I am not

21 Qur'ān, 75:16-17

22 Bukhārī, *k. faḍā'il al-qur'ān, b. khayrukum man ta'llama al-qur'ān wa 'allamahu*, 5027

saying that *alif lām mīm* is one letter; but *alif* is a letter, *lām* is a letter and *mīm* is a letter."[23] As a result of this encouragement, there were hundreds of companions who committed the entire Qur'ān to memory. For example, approximately seventy ḥuffāẓ alone were martyred during the battle of bīr ma'ūnah. These companions in turn were engaged in teaching and spreading the Qur'ān. Through their efforts, the Qur'ān spread throughout the Muslim lands and has been preserved in the chests of Muslims from generation to generation until today.

WRITTEN

There is a common misconception that the Qur'ān was not written during the life of the Prophet ﷺ. Despite the scarcity of people who could read and write, as well as writing materials, the entire Qur'ān was recorded before the Prophet ﷺ left this world. It was not compiled in a single book as it is known today, but it was written on various parchments. There were numerous companions رضي الله عنهم who were appointed as scribes by the Prophet ﷺ. Anas رضي الله عنه narrated that four people from amongst the Anṣār gathered the Qur'ān during the time of the Prophet ﷺ: Ubayy ibn Ka'b, Mu'ādh ibn Jabal, Zaid ibn Thābit, and Abū Zaid رضي الله عنهم. Other reports mention that Abū Bakr, 'Umar, 'Uthmān, and 'Ali رضي الله عنهم were also scribes for the Prophet ﷺ. Every time he received revelation, he would command one of them to write it down.

The Prophet ﷺ would tell his scribes where to place the verses. 'Uthmān (ra) reports that it was the blessed practice of the Prophet ﷺ that soon after the revelation of a certain portion of the Qur'ān, he would pointedly instruct the scribe to write it in a specific surah after a specific verse.[24]

Zaid ibn Thābit رضي الله عنه relates, "I used to write down the words of revelation for the Prophet. When revelation came to him, he would feel intense heat and drops of perspiration would start rolling down his body like pearls. When this state would cease, I would present him with a shoulder-bone or a piece of cloth and begin to write what he would dictate to me... When I was finished, he would say: 'Read'. I would read it back to him. If there was a shortcoming, he would rectify it."[25]

Since paper was scarce during this time, the scribes would write down the verses on whatever they could find. They would write on date palm branches,

---

23 Tirmidhī, *k. faḍā'il al-qur'ān 'an rasūlillah*, 3158

24 Al-Hākim, *Al-Mustadrak*, 2: 221 and Al-Suyūṭī, *Al-Itqān*, 1: 172

25 Al-Hākim, *Al-Mustadrak*, 2: 229

stone slabs, leather scraps, pieces of bamboo, leaves, and animal bones. Basically they would use whatever they could find that was suitable for writing.

Through this method, the entire Qur'ān was written down during the life of the Prophet ﷺ. It was written on various parchments but it was not compiled into one single book as it is today. Similarly, many companions ﷺ had their own personal copies of the Qur'ān that they had written themselves. They would record whatever they heard or memorized from the Prophet ﷺ.

THE ERA OF ABU BAKR ﷺ

During the caliphate of Abū Bakr ﷺ the entire Qur'ān was compiled into a single book. The era of Abū Bakr ﷺ was marked with a lot of difficulties rooted in religious and political strife. There was a war against those who apostatized, those who refused to pay zakāh, and other major battles in which large numbers of companions were martyred. For example, during the battle of Yamāmah[26] alone, over seventy companions who had memorized the Qur'ān were martyred. This created a great level of concern amongst the Muslims, especially amongst the leadership. If the Qurrā' (Reciters) continued to be martyred, some of the knowledge of the Qur'ān would be lost.

'Umar ﷺ brought this concern to Abū Bakr ﷺ and advised him to compile the Qur'ān as a single compilation. Initially, Abū Bakr ﷺ was hesitant to undertake such a monumental task, but eventually agreed to do so after seeing its benefit. He tasked Zaid ibn Thābit ﷺ with the responsibility of compiling the first copy of the Qur'ān.

Zaid ibn Thābit ﷺ narrated the entire incident. "One day, soon after the battle of Yamāmah, Abū Bakr ﷺ sent for me. When I came to meet him, 'Umar ﷺ was present there. Abū Bakr ﷺ said to me, 'Umar ﷺ has just informed me that a large number of huffāẓ (those who had learnt the Qur'ān by heart) have been martyred in the Battle of Yamāmah. If the huffāẓ continue to meet martyrdom in this manner, I am afraid a large portion of the Qur'ān may be lost. So, I propose that you undertake the task of the collection of the Qur'ān from different places. I (Abū Bakr) told 'Umar ﷺ, 'How can I do what the Prophet ﷺ himself did not do?' 'Umar ﷺ replied, 'By Allāh! It is for nothing but good,' and he continued to repeat this statement until the

26 The battle of Yamāmah took place in 12th year after hijrah under the leadership of Khālid ibn Al-Walīd against a group of people who left Islām.

light of its truth dawned upon me as well, and now my opinion is the same as 'Umar's.'

After that Abū Bakr ﵁ said to me (Zaid), 'You are young and sensible. We have no lack of trust in you. You had also been a regular scribe of revelation during the time of the Holy Prophet ﷺ. So search then for all the verses of the Qur'ān and collect them together.'

By Allāh! Carrying a mountain on their orders would have been a lighter burden for me than collecting the Qur'ān. I asked him, 'How is it that you have undertaken a task that was not done by the Prophet ﷺ himself?' Abū Bakr ﵁ said, 'By Allāh! It is but good,' and he kept on repeating these words until Allāh gave me insight to adopt the same opinion held by Abū Bakr and 'Umar. Consequently, I started searching for the verses of the Qur'ān and it was from the branches of date-palms, slabs of stones, and the memory of the people that I finally collected the Qur'ān."[27]

Zaid ﵁ undertook this responsibility with the highest level of care and detail. He established a methodology to follow that had built-in checks and balances to ensure the authenticity of this official copy. Zaid ﵁ himself was a hāfiẓ of the Qur'ān and a scribe of the Prophet ﷺ. If he wanted he could have written the Qur'ān from his own memory. Similarly, there were hundreds of companions who had the Qur'ān memorized and a number who had their own personal copies. Instead of relying on one of these, Zaid ﵁ used a unique combination of all three. Through all three methods, he insured that there was both verbal and written testimony for each verse of the Qur'ān.

A public proclamation was made, calling for written verses of the Qur'ān to be brought to him. When a written verse was brought to him, he would verify its authenticity against his own memory. Then, 'Umar ﵁, who was also a ḥāfiẓ of the Qur'ān and is proven through reliable narrations to have been assigned by Abū Bakr to work with Zaid ﵁ on the project, would test it against his own memory. Written verses would be accepted only if two reliable witnesses testified that they were written in the presence of the Prophet ﷺ. Through this precise and careful method, Zaid ﵁ was able to compile a master copy of the Qur'ān.

In this master copy, the verses were arranged according to the sequence fixed by the Prophet ﷺ. The Surahs were not arranged according to the sequence we know today. Rather, each Surah was written separately in some-

27 Bukhārī, *k. fadā'il al-qur'ān, b. jam' al-qur'ān*, 6:98

thing similar to folders. So each Surah had its own folder.

These folders stayed with Abū Bakr 🙼 until he left this world and were then passed on to 'Umar 🙼. After his martyrdom, they remained with his daughter, the mother of the believers Ḥafṣa 🙼 and were later used by 'Uthmān 🙼 to make official copies.

THE ERA OF 'UTHMAN 🙼

During the Caliphate of 'Uthmān 🙼, Islam had spread far and wide, reaching North West Africa to the West and Iran to the East. The new Muslims of these lands would learn Islam generally and Qur'ān specifically from the Muslim armies, traders, and teachers who came into contact with them. During the early days of the expansion of Islam, Qur'ānic learning and teaching was complicated because it was revealed in "seven recitations". Different companions 🙼 learned the Qur'ān from the Prophet 🙼 in different recitations. These companions then taught it to their students according to the recitation they learned. These companions and their students went to different lands and would teach the recitation they learned. For example, the people of Syria used to read according to the recitation of Ubayy ibn Kaʿb 🙼 and the people of Kufa read according to the recitation of 'Abdullah ibn Masʿūd 🙼. With the spread of Islam, the differences of recitation spread as well. Knowledge of these different recitations was not well known in the new lands, so it started leading to a lot of confusion. It reached to such an extent that people started disputing and arguing with another about the correct recitation of the Qur'ān.

This concern was brought to the attention of 'Uthmān 🙼 who also sensed this was becoming an issue. The incident that led to 'Uthmān's decision to compile a standard copy of the Qur'ān is narrated by Ḥudhaifa ibn Yamān 🙼.

Ḥudhaifah 🙼 noticed that differences were arising amongst people while he was on a military campaign in Azerbaijan. He returned to Madinah and went straight to 'Uthmān 🙼 and said: "O Leader of the Believers! Before this nation falls prey to dissension about the Book of Allāh, like the Jews and Christians, you must do something." 'Uthmān 🙼 asked, "What is the matter?" He replied, "I was on a military mission on the Armenian front where I saw that the recitation of the people of Syria, who follow that of Ubayy ibn

Ka'b 🌸, was not known to the people of Iraq. Similarly, the people of Iraq, who follow the recitation of 'Abdullah ibn Mas'ūd 🌸, had not heard of the recitation of the people of Syria. As a result, they call each other unbelievers."

In response to this concern, 'Uthmān 🌸 called a meeting of the elder Companions and consulted with them. He said, "I have been informed that there are people who say to each other: 'My recitation is better than yours,' and this may be carried to the limits of blasphemy (disbelief). What is your opinion on this matter?" They asked him what he thought. He said, "My opinion is that we should unite everyone on a single transcription so that no difference or division may occur." The Companions approved and supported his view.

'Uthmān 🌸 gathered the people together and addressed them by saying, "You all live so close to me in Madinah and yet repudiate each other and differ with one another in respect of the recitations of the Qur'ān. It is obvious, therefore, that those who are far away from me must be falsifying and disapproving each other much more vehemently. Therefore, let everyone join together to prepare a copy of the Qur'ān to follow that should be obligatory for all."[28]

To carry out this task, 'Uthmān 🌸 appointed four companions: Zaid ibn Thābit, 'Abdullah ibn Zubair, Sa'īd ibn al-'Āṣ, and 'Abd al-Raḥmān ibn Ḥārith ibn Hishām 🌸. He also requested Ḥafṣa 🌸 to lend the copy of the muṣḥaf that was prepared during the time of Abū Bakr 🌸 so that they could use it to make multiple copies. This group of four companions, along with others, carried out this task carefully and methodically, producing a copy of the muṣḥaf that served as the basis for the one we have today.

They used the copy they received from Ḥafṣa 🌸 as the base. However, they did not solely rely on that copy. They adopted the same methodology that Zaid used during the time of Abū Bakr 🌸.

This committee undertook four unique tasks. **Firstly**, the surahs in the copy prepared by Abū Bakr 🌸 were not in sequence. Each Surah was written down separately. They placed the Surahs in the sequence found today in one copy. This sequence was also taught by the Prophet 🌸 through revelation.

Secondly, they wrote the script of the Qur'ān in such a way that it incorporated the different types of recitations. There were no dots or vowel marks placed on the words so that they could be read in accordance with all

---

28   Bukhārī, *k. faḍā'il al-qur'ān, b. jam' al-qur'ān*, 6:99

the valid recitations. For instance, they wrote ننسرها so that it could be read as both ننشرها (*nanshuruha*) and ننشزها (*nunshizuha*) because both the recitations are correct.

Thirdly, they prepared seven copies so that they could be distributed throughout the Muslim world. One stayed in Madinah, one was sent to Makkah, and one each to Syria, Yemen, Bahrain, Basra, and Kufa.

Fourthly, they checked their transcript against the transcript prepared during the time of Abū Bakr ﷺ along with the personal copies of individual companions.

It was the concerns and efforts of Abū Bakr, 'Umar, 'Uthmān, and countless other companions ﷺ that led to the production of the copy of the Qur'ān we have today. Allāh ﷻ chose this blessed generation of people to carry out this monumental task and used them to divinely protect His words. "Indeed, it is We who sent down the Qur'ān and indeed, We will be its guardian."[29]

---

29 Qur'ān, 15: 9

5

SUBJECT MATTER

In Surah Yūsuf, Allāh ﷻ describes the Qurʾān as, "Never was the Qurʾān a narration invented, but a confirmation of what was before it and a detailed explanation of all things and guidance and mercy for a people who believe."[30] The Qurʾān confirms and reaffirms what is mentioned in the scriptures that came before it. Allāh ﷻ Himself says that the Qurʾān is a detailed explanation of every single thing. Ibn Masʿūd رضي الله عنه said, "Whoever wants knowledge then let them turn to the Qurʾān." Imam al-Shāfiʿī said, "Nothing happens to anyone with respect to their religion except that there is guidance for it in the book of Allāh." Once he said, "Ask me about anything and I will tell you about it from the book of Allāh." That is why Ibn 'Abbās رضي الله عنه would say that if I lost my camel's rope, I would find it in the book of Allāh. Meaning that he would look towards the Qurʾān for answers to all of his problems, both big and small.

The primary objective of the Qurʾān is to teach and remind humanity about certain absolute truths and realities that form part of the system of belief of Islām. Basically, it explains the relationship between man and his Creator. The second objective is to detail the rules and regulations that govern everyday life. It provides guidance for life as an individual, as a member of a family, and as a member of society. It provides guidance with respect to

30 Qurʾān, 12:111

social, economic, and political life.

The Qur'ān talks about beliefs, law, history, and parables. It even contains knowledge that is associated with the fields of medicine, debate, astronomy, engineering, algebra, and geology. Although the Qur'ān contains knowledge regarding these sciences and many others, it is not a book of history, science, or medicine. It is primarily a book of guidance. That is why the verses of the Qur'ān discuss four major topics: 1) beliefs, 2) commandments, 3) stories, and 4) parables.

BELIEFS

As mentioned above, one of the primary objectives of the Qur'ān is to teach and remind humanity about certain realities and absolute truths that make up their system of beliefs. That is why Allāh ﷻ addresses three fundamental aspects of belief throughout the Qur'ān: tawḥīd (the oneness of Allāh), risālah (Messengership), and ākhirah (life after death). The Qur'ān deals with these topics extensively in various ways.

Tawḥīd, belief in the oneness of Allāh ﷻ, is the cornerstone of the Islamic creed. This concept is so important that the primary purpose of all Prophets and Messengers was to explain it to their people. Linguistically, the word tawḥīd is the verbal noun from the verb waḥada (وَحَّدَ \ يُوَحِّدُ), which means to make something one, or to assert oneness. When referring to Allāh ﷻ, it is the belief that Allāh ﷻ is One without partner in His dominion, One without similitude in His essence and attributes, and One without rival in His Divinity in worship. It is the belief that Allāh alone is the Creator of the Heavens and the Earth and everything they contain without partner. He alone is the Nourisher, the Sustainer, the One who gives life and death, the Almighty, the All-Powerful, the All-Hearing, the All-Seeing, the All-Knowing and the Controller of all affairs. He alone has the right to be worshipped and He is completely unique. Nothing in this universe resembles Him in any way, shape, or form.

Belief in **prophets and messengers**, risālah, is the second most fundamental principle of faith. It entails believing in and accepting all the prophets and messengers Allāh ﷻ has sent for the guidance of humanity. Starting from Adam ﷺ until the last and final messenger, the seal of prophethood, Muḥammad ﷺ. One must believe in all of them and accept the message they came with as the truth.

The third most fundamental principle of faith is to believe in the **ākhirah**, life after death. One must have firm conviction that the life of this world is temporary and that the life to come is for eternity, and one must believe in resurrection and judgment. One must believe that every single human will be held accountable for what they used to do in the life of this world. It includes belief in the concepts of accountability, reward and punishment, forgiveness and repentance, Paradise and Hell.

The Qur'ān explores these topics in different ways and presents them in different styles so that every sincere human being searching for the truth can find it. It establishes these absolute proofs through various arguments and evidences. Mufti Taqi writes that the Qur'ān uses four unique types of arguments to prove these beliefs: recorded, logical, observational, and experimental.[31]

In addition to proving these three fundamental aspects of belief, the Qur'ān also rejects and answers doubts presented by different groups of people. Specifically, the Qur'ān deals with the false beliefs and doubts of the polytheists, Christians, Jews, and hypocrites.

COMMANDMENTS

The Qur'ān can be thought of as a guidebook for life, the instruction manual given to man in order to teach him how to live life according to the rule of God. In this context, the Qur'ān is a book of law containing both commandments and prohibitions. The verses that talk about law are known as Āyāt al-Aḥkām, or legal verses. There are approximately three hundred and fifty verses that deal with laws. The commandments found in the Qur'ān can be divided into two broad categories: devotional matters ('ibādāt) and civil transactions (mu'āmalāt). Devotional matters are rules that regulate the relationship between man and Creator, and civil transactions are concerned with man and his fellow humans.

There are verses that give basic guidelines for devotional matters such as purification, prayer, fasting, charity, hajj, and sacrifice. These are also classified as the rights of Allāh. The detailed rulings for these acts of worship are found in the Sunnah of the Prophet ﷺ.

31 Usmani, *An Introduction to the Sciences of the Qur'ān*

The verses talking about civil transactions discuss a wide range of subjects including marriage, divorce, paternity, inheritance, and family-law. There are commandments applying to facets of commercial law such as sale, lease, and loan. There are verses that address issues related to criminal law such as murder, highway robbery, theft, drinking, adultery, and slanderous accusation. Other verses deal with matters related to civil law: justice, equality, evidence, consultation, personal rights, and freedoms.

Although the Qur'ān does contain some detailed legal rulings, most legal verses deal with broader principles and concepts. These verses provide general guidelines on every topic of Islamic Law. The details then come in the form of the actions, statements, and tacit approvals of the Prophet ﷺ.

Again, it is important to remember that the Qur'ān is not a legal document even though it contains laws. The vast majority of verses deal with theology, morality, and guidance. The Qur'ān contains verses that regulate social behavior by encouraging kindness, sympathy, compassion, care, forgiveness, love, mercy, patience, forbearance, steadfastness, courage and generosity. Therefore, the Qur'ān provides a complete moral, ethical and legal code for life.

STORIES

Throughout the Qur'ān, Allāh ﷻ relates a number of different events that occurred in the past. The purpose of these stories is not to simply provide information or relate historical facts. Rather the purpose is for the reader or listener to think, reflect, and derive practical morals and lessons. As Allah ﷻ says, "There was certainly in their stories a lesson for those of understanding. Never was the Qur'an a narration invented, but a confirmation of what was before it and a detailed explanation of all things and guidance and mercy for a people who believe."[32] The Qur'ān addresses stories and events of the past through the perspective of guidance. That is why it is very rare to find an entire story mentioned in the Qur'ān from beginning to end with all the little details. It only mentions those parts of the story that can be used to derive points of guidance.

When talking about past stories, the Qur'ān focuses primarily on the Prophets and Messengers. It has mentioned the stories of twenty-five Proph-

32 Qur'ān, 12:111

ets with varying levels of detail from Adam ﷺ until the last and final Messenger Muḥammad ﷺ. The Qur'ān also mentions the stories of certain individuals and past nations. For example, Allāh ﷻ relates the story of the people of the cave[33], the people of the ditch[34], and the people of the town[35]. Oftentimes these stories are mentioned to console, comfort and reassure the Prophet ﷺ in response to the mockery, ridicule and opposition he faced from his own people. Allah ﷻ says in Surah Hūd, "And each [story] We relate to you from the news of the messengers is that by which We make firm your heart. And there has come to you, in this, the truth and an instruction and a reminder for the believers."[36]

Again, the purpose of these stories is not simply to provide historical information or a history lesson. The purpose is to derive moral lessons and general advice for daily life. There are treasures of wisdom hidden in these accounts.

These stories also serve to prove that Muḥammad ﷺ was truthful in his claim to prophethood. The Prophet ﷺ was unlettered; he did not know how to read or write. He had not kept the company of anyone who could teach him these stories. Yet he was still able to accurately narrate the stories of past prophets and nations. This is proof that the words he was reciting were revelation from Allāh.

PARABLES

A parable is defined as a short allegorical story designed to illustrate or teach some truth, religious principle, or moral lesson. The word used for parable in Arabic is mathal, which is translated as an example, metaphor or allegory. Allah ﷻ uses parables throughout the Qur'ān to illustrate or teach some truth, religious principle or moral lesson. Allah ﷻ says in Surah al-Zumar, "And We have certainly presented for the people in this Qur'an from every [kind of] example - that they might remember."[37]

For example, Allah ﷻ says in Surah Ibrāhīm, "Do you not see how Allah makes comparisons (strikes parables)? A good word is like a good tree whose

33 Qur'ān, 18
34 Qur'ān, 85
35 Qur'ān, 36
36 Qur'ān, 11:120
37 Qur'ān, 39:27

root is firm and whose branches are high in the sky, yielding constant fruit by its Lord's leave. Allah makes such comparisons (strikes such parables) for people so that they may reflect."[38] In this verse Allah ﷻ is providing a parable to explain and clarify the concept of faith. Allah compares faith to a date palm. The "good word" is understood to be the declaration of faith, "there is no deity worthy of worship except Allah and Muhammad is the messenger of Allah." The roots of this statement are firmly planted in a believer's heart, the trunk of the tree is the declaration itself, and the branches high in the sky are the various actions and statements that are a result of one's faith. Allah explains faith, which is an abstract concept, by comparing it to a tree.

38 Qur'ān, 14:24

6

MAKKI & MADANI

The Qur'ān was not revealed in a vacuum. In order to understand the message of a verse or surah, it is important to understand its context. The Prophet ﷺ spent a very difficult twelve years in Makkah. People who knew him as the most honest and trustworthy now called him a liar, a forger, a sorcerer, a magician, and even a mad man. He was seen as a direct threat to the status quo. The people who initially accepted Islam were generally weak and poor, and faced persecution at the hands of the Quraysh. After migration, the Muslims gained strength, power, and influence. The issues they dealt with in Madinah were very different than the issues they dealt with in Makkah. That is why there is a noticeable difference in themes and subject matter of revelation before and after migration. This difference in themes and subject matter forms the basis of classifying revelation into Makki and Madani.

WHAT IS MEANT BY MAKKI AND MADANI?

One of the most common ways to classify verses or chapters of the Qur'ān is to classify them into Makki or Madani. That is why the word Makki or Madani is found written next to the title of the surah in most copies of the Qur'ān today. This is a classification based on time, not place.

There is a common misunderstanding that Makki means the surah was revealed in Makkah and Madani means it was revealed in Madinah. This is not the case. Makkan revelation is anything that was revealed before the migration of the Prophet ﷺ from Makkah to Madinah whereas Madani revelation is anything that was revealed after migration. It is a classification based on the time of revelation with migration serving as the determining factor.

The Prophet ﷺ himself did not classify revelation as Makki or Madani, but it was something the Companions regarded as important. They realized that preserving this information was necessary in order for future generations to properly understand the verses. Ibn Masʿūd said, "I swear by Allāh, besides whom there is no other God, there is no Surah in the Qur'ān except that I know where it was revealed." 'Ali said, "By Allāh, I know about every verse whether it was revealed at night or during the day, in the plains or over the mountains."

HOW IS IT KNOWN IF A VERSE OR SURAH IS MAKKI OR MADANI?

There are two primary ways in which the scholars of the Qur'ān determined if a verse or surah is Makki or Madani. The first is through narrations from the Companions. Meaning, a Companion will mention the time and place of a specific verse or surah. Sometimes, they may mention some other information that indicates it was revealed before or after migration. It is important to know that there is not a narration for every single verse of the Qur'ān that describes if it is Makki or Madani.

The second is through educated reasoning based off external factors. Based on the subject matter, style, or theme of the verse or surah, a scholar will conclude if it is Makki or Madani. For example, verses that are addressing the polytheists of Makkah are most likely Makki. Verses that talk about the battle of Badr or hypocrites are most likely Madani. Since this second method is based off of the educated reasoning of a scholar, differences of opinions do arise.

THEMES OF MAKKI AND MADANI REVELATION

The circumstances, conditions, issues, difficulties, and needs of the Prophet ﷺ and the Muslims in Makkah were very different than those in

Madinah. Revelation from Allāh ﷻ took these differences into account. That is why the subject matter, themes, and styles of Makkan revelation are different than those of Madani revelation.

All Makkan revelation shares some common themes. It is important to know that these are generalities and not absolutes. There may be some verses that do not talk about these themes but are still Makki. There may also be some verses that do talk about these themes but are Madani.

THE THEMES OF MAKKAN REVELATION ARE:

1. The three fundamental aspects of Islamic Belief: The oneness of Allāh ﷻ, prophethood, and life after death. The establishment of these beliefs is the most common theme of Makkan revelation. It talks about the oneness of Allāh ﷻ, His names and attributes, omnipotence, and ultimate power. It mentions the stories of the Prophets and Messengers and the difficulties they faced in inviting others towards faith. It proves the reality and certainty of resurrection, life after death, reward, and punishment. It rejects the false beliefs of those who associate partners with Allah ﷻ.
2. Morality in general: The Makkan verses discuss what is considered to be good, upright moral behavior in a person's speech and action, and reject immoral practices prevalent in pre-Islamic society.
3. Stories of past prophets, messengers, and nations: The main purpose of these stories is for the reader to derive morals, lessons, and reminders.

THE THEMES OF MADANI REVELATION ARE:

1. Ritual acts of worship such as prayer, fasting, hajj, and charity. The verses discuss the general obligations and the details are found in the Sunnah of the Prophet ﷺ.
2. Rulings and regulations related to personal, social, and economic life. For example, marriage and divorce, war, the permissibility of sales, the prohibition of interest, the laws concerning punishments, and the rules of inheritance. This is in no way meant to be an exhaustive list, but it gives a general idea.
3. Discussions with the Jews, Christians, and hypocrites regarding their beliefs and how to interact with them. These verses discuss

the false beliefs that crept into Judaism and Christianity and invites them back to Islam.

CHARACTERISTICS OF MAKKI AND MADANI REVELATION

Makki and Madani revelation also have very distinct characteristics in terms of language, sound, and style. After analyzing both types of verses and surahs, scholars developed lists detailing these differences in characteristics.

THE CHARACTERISTICS OF MAKKI SURAHS ARE:

1. Usage of the word كَلَّا, which means "No! Never!"
2. Beginning with the broken letters, except for Surah al-Baqarah and Surah Āli ʿImrān.
3. The presence of a verse of prostration.
4. Mention of the story of Adam and Satan except for Surah al-Baqarah.
5. Brevity and rhythm; Makkan verses are generally shorter and can have a rhyming sound.
6. The use of oaths.

THE CHARACTERISTICS OF MADANI VERSES ARE:

1. The mention of specific punishments for certain crimes.
2. The mention of hypocrites, Jews, and Christians.
3. Length; Madani verses are generally longer.

HOW VERSES AND SURAHS ARE CLASSIFIED AS MAKKI OR MADANI

The Qurʾān was revealed gradually over a period of twenty-three years. Often times, surahs were not revealed in their entirety. Sometimes a few verses would be revealed, while other times a single verse or even a portion of a verse would be revealed. There are surahs that were revealed entirely before migration, some after, and some in both. There are surahs in which the majority of verses are Makki but a few are Madani and others that are Madani with a few Makki. When it comes to labeling a surah as Makki or Madani, scholars considered the majority of the verses. Due to this, the scholars of 'Ulūm al-Qur'ān developed the following classifications:

1. Makki Surahs: The majority of verses were revealed before migration. There might be some verses that are Madani.
2. Madani Surahs: The majority of verses were revealed after migration. There might be some verses that are Makki.
3. A difference of opinion exists regarding whether the Surah is Makki or Madani.

IMPORTANCE

The knowledge of whether a surah is Makki or Madani is important in several ways. For example, context is extremely important for developing a proper understanding of a person's words and statements. Taking verses of the Qur'ān out of their proper context can lead to a lot of misunderstanding, even for Muslims. Having knowledge of whether a verse or surah is Makki or Madani provides that context. It gives a framework on how to approach and understand the subject matter and themes of the surah.

In addition to providing context this knowledge assists in understanding the concept of abrogation (discussed in chapter eight). It also gives insight into the life of the Prophet ﷺ, his companions ﵃, and the issues and problems they came across in the various stages of the sīrah.

7

CAUSES OF REVELATION

The main purpose of revelation is guidance: to guide humanity from the darkness of disbelief to the light of faith, from immorality to morality. As Allāh ﷻ says, "A book that We have revealed to you to remove people from darkness to light."[39]

As mentioned before, the Qur'an was revealed in portions over a period of twenty three years. Sometimes a single verse would be revealed. Other times a set of verses, or even an entire surah were revealed. Often the revelation would come in response to a certain situation, event, problem, or question posed to the Prophet ﷺ. That situation, event, problem, or question is known as the Sabab al-Nuzūl, or the cause of revelation. It has been defined as the background for the revelation -- the event, occurrence, or question that was the direct cause of revelation of a verse or surah.

Having knowledge of the causes of revelation plays a major role in providing a proper understanding of the meaning of a verse. That is why, historically, scholars have always given importance to studying the narrations that mention a cause of revelation and even compiled those narrations into books.

EXAMPLES

39 Qur'ān, 14:1

An example of such a narration is found in Ṣaḥīḥ al-Bukhārī. Khabbāb ibn al-Arat 🌸 narrated, "I was a blacksmith and al-ʿĀṣ ibn Wāʾil owed me a debt, so I went to him to demand it. He said to me, 'I will not pay you your debt until you disbelieve in Muḥammad.' I said, 'I will not disbelieve in Muḥammad until you die and then be resurrected.' He said, 'Will I be resurrected after my death? If so, I shall pay you (there) if I should find wealth and children.' So it was revealed, 'Have you seen him who disbelieved in Our Signs, and yet says: I shall certainly be given wealth and children? Has he, known to the unseen or has he taken a covenant from (Allāh) the Beneficent? Nay! We shall record what he says, and we shall add and add to his punishment. And We shall inherit from him all that he talks of, and he shall appear before Us alone.'"[40]

Another example is the ḥadīth narrated by al-Barāʾ 🌸. He narrated, "The Prophet 🌸 prayed facing Bayt al-Maqdis for sixteen or seventeen months but he wished that his qiblah would be the Kaʿbah. So Allāh Revealed (2:144) and he offered ʿAṣr prayer and some people prayed with him. A man from among those who had prayed with him, went out and passed by some people offering prayer in another mosque, and they were in the state of bowing. He said, 'I testify that I have prayed with the Prophet 🌸 facing Makkah.' Hearing that, they turned their faces to the Kaʿbah while they were still bowing. Some men had died before the Qiblah was changed towards the Kaʿbah. They had been killed and we did not know what to say about them (i.e. whether their prayers towards Jerusalem were accepted or not). So Allāh revealed, 'And Allāh would never make your faith (i.e. prayer) to be lost (i.e. your prayers offered towards Jerusalem). Truly Allāh is Full of Pity, Most Merciful towards mankind.'"[41]

It is important to note that not every single verse of the Qurʾān has a cause of revelation. As a matter of fact, the majority of verses were revealed without having a specific cause associated with them. That is why there are two types of verses with respect to causes of revelation: 1) those that do not have a specific cause and 2) those that have a specific cause.

IMPORTANCE

---

40   Bukhārī, *k. al-tafsīr*, 4735
41   Bukhārī, *k. al-imān, b. al-salah min al-imān*, 33

As mentioned earlier, knowing the cause of revelation plays an important role in shaping a proper understanding of a verse. As a matter of fact, it is safe to say that some verses cannot be understood properly without knowing why it was revealed. Al-Wāḥidi ☸ wrote, "It is not possible to know the explanation of a verse without being aware of its story and how it was revealed."

The scholars of 'Ulūm Al-Qur'ān have listed a few benefits of knowing the causes of revelation:

1. It sheds light on the wisdom behind a particular legal ruling.
2. It provides context and background that will prevent misinterpretations.
3. It aids in properly applying the verse.
4. It provides the names of individuals who may be referred to in a verse.

IS CONSIDERATION GIVEN TO THE WORDS' GENERAL MEANINGS OR THE SPECIFIC CAUSE?

The scholars have disagreed regarding a very fine issue: when interpreting a verse, should consideration be given to the general meanings of the words or the specific cause of revelation? Meaning, if a particular incident occurred and a verse was revealed regarding it, should the ruling of that verse be limited to that specific incident or can it be applied generally?

The vast majority of scholars agree that consideration is given to the general meanings of words. Imam Al-Suyūṭī ☸ writes in Al-Itqān fi 'Ulūm Al-Qur'ān, "From the proofs that consideration is for the general meanings of words is that the Companions ☸ and others used the general meanings of verses as proofs even though they were revealed with a specific cause."[42] In easier words, the application of a verse is general and is not limited to the specific incident that was its cause of revelation.

---

42   Al-Suyūṭī, *Al-Itqān fī 'ulūm al-qur'ān*

8

ABROGATION

AL-NASKH

Islam provides the most complete and comprehensive legal code of life that is suitable for all times and places. There is deep divine wisdom in the Sharī'ah, the moral, ethical, and legal code of Islam. Every single command, prohibition, or recommendation was revealed to either provide benefit to humanity or to remove some type of harm. Sometimes this divine wisdom is apparent and easy to understand, and sometimes the human intellect is not able to recognize these wisdoms.

The entire Sharī'ah was not revealed all at once. Part of the divine wisdom of Allāh ﷻ was to reveal the laws of Islam gradually so that it would be easy for people to accept and act upon them. That is why there are some things that may have been permissible or recommended in the earlier days of Islam that were later on made impermissible or disliked. Lifting a particular ruling and replacing it with another is known as naskh.

DEFINITION

Linguistically the word naskh is derived from the verb nasakha (نَسَخَ), which carries several meanings. It can mean to delete, abrogate, repeal, remove, transfer from one place to another, or to change.

Technically, it refers to the abrogation of a legal ruling by another legal ruling that was revealed after it. Basically, Allāh ﷻ may enforce a law that is relevant for a certain time and place. Then, in His infinite wisdom, He repeals that law and replaces it with a new one. The abrogated ruling is called mansūkh and the abrogating ruling is called nāsikh. This process is known as naskh.

PROOF OF ABROGATION

Allāh ﷻ says in Surah al-Baqarah, "We do not abrogate a verse or cause it to be forgotten except that We bring forth [one] better than it or similar to it. Do you not know that Allāh is over all things competent?"[43]

This particular verse was revealed in response to an objection raised by the Jews of Madinah. They would ask each other, "Are you not surprised by Muḥammad's affair? He commands his companions to do something then he prohibits them and tells them to do its opposite. Today he says something, then changes it tomorrow. This Qur'ān is nothing but the speech of Muḥammad that he created himself." So Allāh ﷻ revealed this noble verse as a response to their ignorant objection.

Similarly, Allāh ﷻ says in Surah al-Naḥl, "And when We substitute a verse in place of a verse - and Allāh is most knowing of what He sends down - they say, 'You, [O Muḥammad], are but an inventor [of lies].' But most of them do not know. Say, [O Muḥammad], 'The Pure Spirit has brought it down from your Lord in truth to make firm those who believe and as guidance and good tidings to the Muslims.'"[44]

EXAMPLES

Initially after migration, the Muslims were commanded to face Bayt al-Maqdis in Jerusalem for prayer. After a short while, this command was abrogated and the Prophet ﷺ and the Muslims were told to face the Kaʿbah in Makkah for prayer. Allāh ﷻ says, "We have certainly seen the turning of your face, [O Muḥammad], toward the heaven, and We will surely turn you to a qiblah with which you will be pleased. So turn your face toward al-Masjid al-Haram. And wherever you [believers] are, turn your faces toward it [in

43 Qur'ān, 2:106

44 Qur'ān, 16:101-102

prayer]."[45] Allāh ﷻ even mentions how the non-believers would raise objections to this. "The foolish among the people will say, 'What has turned them away from their qiblah, which they used to face?' Say, 'To Allāh belongs the east and the west. He guides whom He wills to a straight path.'"[46]

Another example is the ruling regarding the waiting period of a widow. Initially, the waiting period was set as one complete year. Allāh ﷻ says, "And those who are taken in death among you and leave wives behind - for their wives is a bequest: maintenance for one year without turning [them] out."[47] This ruling was later abrogated and changed to four months and ten days. "And those who are taken in death among you and leave wives behind - they, [the wives, shall] wait four months and ten [days]."[48]

TYPES OF ABROGATION

There are three types of abrogation that take place in the Qur'ān:

1. Abrogation of the recitation and the ruling.
2. Abrogation of the recitation and not the ruling.
3. Abrogation of the ruling and not the recitation.

ABROGATION OF THE RECITATION AND THE RULING

In this type of abrogation, the verse is no longer a part of the Qur'ān, nor is its ruling applicable. It is complete abrogation. An example of this has been narrated by 'Ā'ishah رضي الله عنها. She narrated, "It had been revealed in the Qur'ān that ten sucklings made marriage unlawful. This was later abrogated by five sucklings, and the Prophet ﷺ passed away and before that it was recited in the Qur'ān."[49]

In this narration, 'Ā'ishah رضي الله عنها explicitly mentioned that there used to be a verse that talked about nursing and its quantity that was later abrogated. This narration also shows that 'Ā'ishah رضي الله عنها was familiar with the concept of abrogation and that it was not something strange.

45 Qur'ān, 2:144
46 Qur'ān, 2:142
47 Qur'ān, 2:240
48 Qur'ān, 2:234
49 Muslim, *k. al-riḍā', b. al-taḥrīm bi khams raḍ'āt*, 1452

ABROGATION OF THE RECITATION AND NOT THE RULING

In this type of abrogation, the verse is no longer a part of the Qur'ān but its ruling is still applicable. It is partial abrogation and one that is difficult for people to understand. An example of this is the ruling of stoning the male and female adulterer.

'Umar ﷺ while giving a sermon in the Prophet's ﷺ mosque said, "Verily, Allāh sent Muḥammad ﷺ with the truth, and He sent the book down upon him. The verse of stoning was revealed with it; we recited it, memorized it, and understood it. The Prophet ﷺ awarded the punishment of stoning to death, and after him we did the same. I am afraid that with the passage of time, people will forget it and say, 'We do not find the punishment of stoning in the Book of Allāh,' and go astray by abandoning this duty prescribed by Allāh. Stoning is a duty laid down in Allāh's book for married men and women who commit adultery when proof is established."[50]

This narration establishes that there was a verse in the Qur'ān that mentioned the punishment of stoning. This verse was later abrogated but the ruling remained intact. Another narration actually preserves the wording of that particular abrogated verse.

ABROGATION OF THE RULING AND NOT THE RECITATION

In this type of abrogation the verse is still part of the Qur'ān but the ruling derived from it is no longer applicable. So it is also a type of partial abrogation. There are numerous examples of this type of abrogation because it is the most common form found in the Qur'ān.

An example of this is the waiting period that has been prescribed for a widow. Initially the waiting period was prescribed as one full year. As Allāh ﷻ says in Surah al-Baqarah, "And those who are taken in death among you and leave wives behind - for their wives is a bequest: maintenance for one year without turning [them] out."[51] Later this ruling was abrogated and changed to four months and ten days. Allāh ﷻ says, "And those who are taken in death among you and leave wives behind - they, [the wives, shall] wait four months and ten [days]."[52] Although the ruling of the first verse has been abrogated, the verse is still part of the Qur'ān.

---

50 Muslim, *k. al-hudūd, b. rajm al-thayyib fi al-zina*

51 Qur'ān, 2:240

52 Qur'ān, 2:234

IMPORTANCE

The knowledge of abrogation including which verses have been abrogated and which verses did the abrogation is extremely important for having a proper understanding of the rulings of the Qur'ān. There is no way for a person to interpret or understand the Qur'ān without having knowledge of abrogation.

9

THE SEVEN LETTERS & THE DIFFERENT RECITATIONS

It is a well-established fact that the dialects of different people speaking the same language can differ drastically from place to place. The English spoken in California sounds different than the English spoken in Texas, New York, or Boston in terms of accent, pronunciation, and even usage of words. There are differences even between Southern California and Northern California.

While in Makkah the majority of Muslims were from the same background and spoke the same Qurayshi dialect, as Islam expanded throughout the Arabian Peninsula it came into contact with people who spoke other Arabic dialects. Teaching them the Qur'ān was a necessity but asking them to leave their native dialect would have been difficult. Therefore the Prophet ﷺ taught them in their own dialects and that is why the Qur'ān was revealed in seven letters: to facilitate greater ease in both recitation and memorization.

THE SEVEN LETTERS

The Qur'ān was revealed in seven letters. There is a great deal of disagreement regarding what these "seven letters" mean exactly. As a starting point, it can be said that the Aḥruf are the various ways that the verses of the Qur'ān are read.

The proof of the Qur'ān being revealed in seven letters or seven dialects is found in many narrations of the Prophet ﷺ, so much so that it reaches the level of tawātur. Jalāl al-Dīn al-Suyūṭī ﷺ lists twenty-one companions who narrated that the Qur'ān was revealed in seven letters.

A FEW NARRATIONS REGARDING THE SEVEN LETTERS

Ibn 'Abbās ﷺ reported that the Prophet ﷺ said, "Jibrīl recited the Qur'ān to me in one ḥarf, and I recited it back to him, but I requested him to increase the number of ḥurūf and he continued to increase it for me, until we stopped at seven Aḥruf." Ibn Shihāb, one of the narrators said, "It has reached me that these seven Aḥruf are essentially one in meaning; they do not differ about what is permitted or forbidden."[53]

'Umar ibn al-Khattāb ﷺ narrated, "I was sitting in the masjid when I heard Hishām ibn Ḥakīm recite Surah al-Furqān. I was about to jump on him in his prayer, but I waited until he finished, and then grabbed him by his garment and asked him, 'Who taught you to recite in such a manner?' He replied, 'It was the Prophet ﷺ himself.' I responded, 'You are mistaken, for indeed I learned this surah from the Prophet ﷺ and it was different from your recitation.' Therefore, I dragged him to the Prophet ﷺ and complained to him that Hishām had recited Surah al-Furqān in a manner different from what he ﷺ had taught me. At this the Prophet ﷺ told me to let go of Hishām and asked him to recite Surah al-Furqān. Hishām recited the Surah in the same way I had heard him before. When he finished the Prophet ﷺ said, 'It was revealed this way.' He then asked me to recite the same Surah. When I finished he said, 'It was also revealed this way. Indeed, the Qur'ān has been revealed in seven different letters, so recite whichever one is easy for you.'"[54]

Ubayy in Ka'b ﷺ narrates that once the Prophet ﷺ met Jibrīl and said, "O Jibrīl! I have been sent to an illiterate nation. Among them are old and young men and women, and those who have never read any writing!" Jibrīl replied, "O Muḥammad, the Qur'ān has been revealed in seven letters."[55]

It is clear from these narrations that the main reason why the Qur'ān was revealed in seven letters was to facilitate the recitation and memorization of

53 Bukhārī, k. *fadā'il al-qur'ān, b. unzila al-qur'ān 'ala sab'ati ahruf,* 4991

54 Bukhārī, k. *fadā'il al-qur'ān, b. unzila al-qur'ān 'ala sab'ati ahruf,* 4992

55 Tirmidhī, k. *al-qira'āt 'an rasūlillah,* 3196

the Qur'ān.

WHAT ARE THE SEVEN LETTERS?

There are several opinions regarding what is actually meant by the seven letters. The most common and widely accepted opinion is that the seven letters refer to the seven dialects (lughāt) of the Arabs prevalent at the time of the Prophet ﷺ. Each of these dialects belongs to a tribe of the Arabs. These tribes are the Quraysh, Hudhayl, Tamīm, Hawāzin, Thaqīf, Kinānah, and Yemen. Meaning, various verses would be pronounced according to the pronunciation of the particular tribe.

Another popular opinion is that the "seven letters" refer to seven different types of variations that may occur in certain verses. The seven variations are the following:

1. Differences in word structure from singular to plural, or masculine to feminine. For example, in one recitation a portion of verse 57 from Surah al-Nisā' is read "lī amānātihim" using the plural and in another recitation it is read "lī amānatihim" using the singular.
2. Variances in verb tenses; past, present, or command.
3. Slight variances in the sequence of letters or words. Meaning switching one letter for another or one word for another. For example, according to one recitation verse 5 of Surah al-Qāriʿah is "ka al-ʿihn al-manfūsh" and in another it is "ka al-ṣūf al-manfūsh."
4. Slight differences in word order.
5. Differences in vowels markings.
6. The addition or subtraction of a letter or word.
7. Slight differences in pronunciation.

None of these variations would affect the meanings of the verses and are all considered to be a part of the Qur'ān.

THE DIFFERENT RECITATIONS

Linguistically, the word Qira'āt is the plural of the word Qirā'ah, which comes from the verb *qara'a* (قَرَأَ), which means to read or to recite. The word

Qirā'ah means recitation. Technically, when used with the Qur'ān it refers to the different ways and manners of reciting the Qur'ān. They can be thought of as unique styles of recitation that are named after the reciters who recited the Qur'ān in that unique style. They represent the various ways in which the Companions ﷺ learned the Qur'ān from the Prophet ﷺ.

It is important to note that the seven letters are distinct from the different recitations of the Qur'ān. Although they are closely related, they are two different things. The different recitations have preserved the ways that the Prophet ﷺ taught his companions to recite the Qur'ān.

10

TAFSIR

Amongst all of the various subjects studied within the Sciences of the Qurʾān, tafsīr is the most important. Tafsīr is the key to unlocking how to understand and implement the Qurʾān properly, which is the primary purpose of this branch of knowledge.

As mentioned earlier, the recitation of the Qurʾān itself is a great act of worship that carries a lot of rewards, virtues, and blessings. However, the actual purpose of the Qurʾān is to think, reflect, ponder, and contemplate over its meanings. As Allāh ﷻ says in Surah Ṣād, "A blessed Book that We have revealed to you, [O Muḥammad], that they might reflect upon its verses, and that those of understanding would be reminded."[56] The only way to contemplate and reflect over its words and meanings is to actually know what those words and meanings are, and that is learned through tafsīr. That is why learning tafsīr is considered to be an obligation upon every Muslim in varying degrees. One way to look at it is that the Qurʾān is a treasure chest full of guidance and wisdom. The key to unlocking that chest is tafsīr.

DEFINITION

Linguistically, tafsīr is a verbal noun from the verb *fassara* (فَسَّرَ), which

56 Qur'ān, 38:29

means to explain, expound, make clear, or interpret. The word tafsīr means "the explanation or interpretation of something." Technically, it refers to the science by which the Qur'ān is understood, its meanings are explained, and its rulings and wisdoms are derived. It is a branch of knowledge in which the meanings of the Qur'ān are explained and its injunctions and wisdoms are described openly and clearly.

IMPORTANCE

The importance of tafsīr cannot be overemphasized. The words of the Qur'ān are so powerful, so awe-inspiring, so deep and heavy in meaning that if they were to be revealed on a mountain it would crumble and turn into dust. As Allāh ﷻ says, "Had we sent down this Qur'ān to a mountain, you would have seen it humbled, bursting apart out of awe for Allāh."[57] A mountain is the largest and strongest naturally occurring physical structure. It is a symbol of power and strength. If the words of Allāh can cause a mountain to humble itself, crumble and break apart out of the fear of Allāh, imagine the effect it can have on the human heart.

History has witnessed the transformative power of these words. These are the same words that when recited to the Companions ﷺ raised them from being nomadic tribesmen to sitting on the thrones of the Roman and Persian Empires. These words elevated them from ignorance to knowledge, from disgrace to honor, and from darkness to light. These are the same words that caused the greatest enemies of Islam to sneak out in the middle of the night and secretly listen to the Prophet ﷺ reciting them. These are the same words that caused the non-believers of Makkah to fall down in prostration. The same words that conquered the heart of ʿUmar ؓ, converting the enraged, would-be assassin of the Prophet ﷺ into one of his most stalwart followers. The same words that when the verses prohibiting alcohol were revealed, almost instantly the streets of Madinah were flowing with the alcohol discarded by the Companions. The science of Tafsīr is meant to explain and open the power of Allāh's words.

Imām al-Suyūṭī ؒ captured the importance of tafsīr beautifully when he wrote, "(The science of tafsīr) is the most honorable of all sciences for three reasons. The first reason is with respect to its topic. It deals with the Speech

57 Qur'ān, 59:21

of Allāh, which contains every kind of wisdom and virtue. It contains pronouncements about what has passed, reports of what will happen, and judgments concerning what happens between people. Its wonders never cease. The second reason is with respect to its goal. Its goal is to lead mankind to the firm handhold of Allāh and to true happiness that does not end. The third reason is with respect to the great need for this science. Every aspect of this religion and this world in the near or distant future is in need of the sciences of the Shariah and knowledge of the religion. This knowledge can only be obtained by understanding the book of Allāh."[58]

SOURCES OF TAFSIR

Part of the responsibility of the Prophet ﷺ was to recite the Qur'ān to the people and to explain its meanings. The Prophet ﷺ would teach them both the words and meanings of the Qur'ān. As Allāh ﷻ says in Surah Āli-'Imran, "Certainly did Allāh confer [great] favor upon the believers when He sent among them a Messenger from themselves, reciting to them His verses and purifying them and teaching them the Book and wisdom, although they had been before in manifest error."[59] Similarly Allāh ﷻ says, "[We sent them] with clear proofs and written ordinances. And We revealed to you the message that you may make clear to the people what was sent down to them and that they might give thought."[60] So the Prophet ﷺ not only taught the words of the Qur'ān to the people but he also explained their meanings in detail.

The Companions had another advantage. During the life of the Prophet ﷺ they witnessed the revelation of the Qur'ān with their own eyes. They were aware of the background, circumstances, reasons, and events surrounding revelation. The Arabic of the Qur'ān was their native language. They understood the usage of words, their connotations, and various nuances of meanings. If any of the Companions ﷺ faced some difficulty in understanding the Qur'ān, they would simply turn to the Prophet ﷺ. Thus, as long as the Prophet ﷺ graced this world with his noble presence, understanding and interpreting the Qur'ān did not pose much of a problem.

After the Prophet ﷺ left this world, his Companions ﷺ, who learned

58 Al-Suyūṭī, *Al-Itqān fi 'ulūm al-qur'ān*
59 Qur'ān, 3:164
60 Qur'ān, 6:44

the Qurʾān and its meanings directly from him, took on the responsibility of explaining the Qurʾān. They taught the Qurʾān to their students, the generation known as the Successors, who then taught it to their students using the same methodology employed by their teachers, the companions.

However, as time passed, it became necessary that a proper way of interpreting and understanding the Qurʾān also be preserved so that the Qurʾān would not become a playground for people's own ideas, philosophies, worldviews, and desires. It was necessary so that people could not interpret the Qurʾān as they pleased. The Qurʾān is divinely protected and part of that divine protection is to ensure that the original meanings and intent are preserved as well.

It is for this reason that a proper methodology for interpreting the Qurʾān was developed through the first three or four generations of Islam. Imām al-Suyūṭī ﷺ summarized this methodology saying, "The scholars have said: Whoever wishes to interpret the Qurʾān, he should first turn to the Qurʾān itself. This is because what has been narrated briefly in one place might be explained in detail in another place, and what is summarized in one place might be explained in another... If he has done that then he turns to the Sunnah, for it is the explainer of the Qurʾān and its clarifier. Imam al-Shāfʿī said, 'All that the Prophet ﷺ said is based on his understanding of the Qurʾān.' And Allāh said, 'Verily We have revealed to you the book in truth so that you may judge between mankind by that which Allāh has shown you.' And the Prophet ﷺ said, 'Indeed, I have been given the Qurʾān and something similar to it,' meaning the Sunnah. If he does not find it in the Sunnah, he turns to the statements of the Companions for they are the most knowledgeable of it since they witnessed the circumstances and situations the Qurʾān was revealed in and since they were blessed with complete understanding, true knowledge, and pious actions."[61]

Scholars have expounded on this and listed out six primary sources of tafsīr: 1) the Qurʾān, 2) sunnah, 3) narrations of Companions, 4) narrations of Successors, 5) Arabic language and poetry, and 6) personal interpretation. Each of these is discussed below in detail.

TAFSIR OF QUR'AN BY QUR'AN

61 Al-Suyūṭī, *Al-Itqān fī 'ulūm al-qur'ān*

The primary source of tafsīr is the Qur'ān itself. Sometimes Allāh ﷻ will mention something briefly and provide the details somewhere else. Sometimes a question will be asked and then answered. Sometimes a story is mentioned briefly and its details are mentioned later on.

For example, Allāh ﷻ says in Surah al-Fātiḥah, "Guide us to the straight path, the path of those you have blessed."[62] The question arises, who are those that Allāh ﷻ has blessed? Who exactly is He referring to in the verse? Allāh ﷻ answers the question in Surah al-Nisa: "and whoever obeys Allāh and His messenger, they will be in the company of those whom Allāh has blessed, of the Prophets, and the truthful followers, and the martyrs, and the pious."[63]

Another example is when Allāh ﷻ says in Surah al-Baqarah, "Then Adam received from His Lord words, and He accepted his repentance."[64] The question comes to mind, what were these words of repentance? Allāh ﷻ mentions them in Surah al-'Arāf, "They said, 'Our Lord! We have wronged ourselves. If you do not forgive us and have mercy on us, we will be of the lost.'"[65]

TAFSIR OF QUR'AN BY SUNNAH

The second source of tafsīr is the normative practice of the Prophet ﷺ or his sunnah. The Prophet ﷺ was a walking example of the Qur'ān; he personified its message through his speech, actions, behavior, character, and morals. It is impossible to have a proper understanding of the Qur'ān without the practical example of the Prophet ﷺ. The Sunnah is necessary for having a correct and complete understanding of the Qur'ān.

One of the primary responsibilities of the Prophet ﷺ as the last and final messenger was to explain and clarify the meanings of the Qur'ān. As Allāh ﷻ says, "And we revealed to you the message that you may make clear to the people what was sent down to them and that they might give thought."[66] This verse makes it clear that the Prophet ﷺ was given the responsibility of teaching the meanings of the Qur'ān. When he would teach the companions how to read the actual words of the Qur'ān, he taught them the meanings as well.

Sometimes the Prophet ﷺ would mention the explanation of a partic-

62 Qur'ān, 1:7
63 Qur'ān, 4:69
64 Qur'ān, 2:37
65 Qur'ān, 7:23
66 Qur'ān, 16:44

ular verse, then mention the verse that he was referring to with his explanation. Abū Hurairah ﷺ narrated that the Messenger of Allāh ﷺ said, "When Allāh loves a slave He calls, 'O Jibrīl! Indeed I love so-and-so, so love him.'" He said: "So he calls out in the heavens. Then love for him descends among the people of the earth. That is the saying of Allāh: 'Verily, those who believe and work deeds of righteousness, the Most Gracious will grant love for them,' (19:96) And when Allāh hates a slave He calls out, 'O Jibrīl! Indeed I hate so-and-so.' So he calls out in the heavens. Then hatred for him descends upon the earth."[67]

Sometimes the Companions would find a verse difficult to understand so he would explain it to them. For example, when the verse "They who believe and do not mix their belief with injustice" was revealed, the Companions ﷺ found it difficult to understand. So they came to the Prophet ﷺ and asked, "O Messenger of Allāh, who amongst us does not do injustice to themselves?" The Prophet ﷺ replied, "It is not that. It is referring to shirk. Have you not heard what Luqmān said to his son while advising him, "O my son, do not associate [anything] with Allāh. Indeed, association [with him] is great injustice."[68]

There are many more examples of the Prophet ﷺ explaining the meanings of the Qur'ān to his companions ﷺ. What is important to keep in mind is that he ﷺ was sent as a teacher. If Allāh ﷺ wanted, He could have simply revealed the Qur'ān to the people of Quraysh as a book of guidance and expect them to accept it, read it, and act upon it themselves. Instead, He chose to send the Prophet ﷺ as a teacher along with it. His entire essence was the embodiment of the teachings of the Qur'ān. That is why when 'Ā'ishah ﷺ was asked about his character she replied, "His character was the Qur'ān."

TAFSIR OF QUR'AN BY THE NARRATIONS OF COMPANIONS ﷺ

The third source of tafsīr is narrations from the companions of the Prophet ﷺ. The Companions ﷺ are considered to be the best generation of people to walk on the face of this Earth after the prophets and messengers. As the Prophet ﷺ said, "The best of generations is my generation. Then the one

---

67 Tirmidhī, k. *tafsīr al-qur'ān 'an rasūlillah*, 3457

68 Bukhārī, k. *ahādīth al-anbiyā', b. qawl allah wattakhadha Allāhu ibrāhīma khalīla*, 3360

after it and the one after it."[69] They were chosen by Allāh ﷻ to be the companions of the Prophet ﷺ and to spread Islam. Both Allāh and His messenger testified to their character and religious knowledge.

Their narrations are considered to be a source of tafsīr for several reasons. The Qur'ān was revealed to their nation. They witnessed the revelation of the Qur'ān first-hand and understood the circumstances in which it was revealed. They understood what problems it was addressing as well as who it was addressing. Often times, verses were revealed in response to problems they dealt with personally. In addition, the Qur'ān was revealed in their native language. They were familiar with how the language functioned, the meanings of words, and various nuances.

They would search for the explanation of words and verses in the Qur'ān, the sunnah of the Prophet ﷺ, and often times the language itself. They would see how the word was used, what it meant in different contexts, and what connotations it carried. For example, 'Ali رضي الله عنه explained that the words "and by the roof raised high"[70] is referring to the sky. As proof, he recited the verse, "And We made the sky a protected ceiling, but they, from its signs, are turning away."[71] This is an example of how a companion would use the Qur'ān to explain the Qur'ān.

There were a number of Companions who were well known for their in-depth knowledge and understanding of the Qur'ān. Imam al-Suyūṭī wrote, "There are ten who were famous for their knowledge of tafsīr amongst the Companions: the four Khulafā' al-Rāshidūn, 'Abdullah ibn Masʿūd, 'Abdullah ibn 'Abbās, Ubay ibn Kaʿb, Zaid ibn Thābit, Abū Musa al-Ashʿarī, and 'Abdullah ibn Zubair."[72] ʿAbdullah ibn 'Abbās was considered to be the most knowledgeable when it came to the interpretation of the Qur'ān. ʿAbdullah ibn 'Umar رضي الله عنه said, "Ibn 'Abbās is the most knowledgeable of this Ummah concerning the revelation given to Muḥammad ﷺ."

TAFSIR OF QUR'AN BY THE NARRATIONS OF SUCCESSORS

رحمهم الله

The fourth source of tafsīr is the narrations of the tābiʿūn, the students

69 Bukhārī, *k. al-riqāq, b. mā yuhadharu min zaharah al-dunya wa al-tanāfusi fīha*, 6429
70 Qur'ān, 52:5
71 Tafseer Al-Tabari (18/27)
72 Al-Suyūṭī, *Al-Itqān fi ʿUlūm Al-Qur'ān*

of the Companions ﷺ. The Successors learned the Qur'ān directly from the Companions of the Prophet ﷺ. They are included in the statement of the Prophet ﷺ, "The best of generations is my generation. Then the one after it and the one after it."[73]

There were a number of luminaries amongst them who were known for their in-depth knowledge and understanding of the Qur'ān. For example, Qatādah said, "There is not a single verse in the Qur'ān except that I have heard something about it." Similarly, Mujāhid is quoted to have said, "I recited the Qur'ān to Ibn 'Abbas three times, and in each recitation, I stopped at every verse asking him about its Tafsīr."

The Successors had developed a certain methodology for interpreting and explaining the Qur'ān built upon the methodology of their teachers, the Companions. Their primary source for explaining the meanings of the Qur'ān was the Qur'ān itself. If they could not find the explanation in the Qur'ān, they would turn to the Sunnah of the Prophet ﷺ. If they could not find it there, they would look to the narrations of the Companions. If they still could not find it, then they would look to the language itself and use their own intellect to arrive at a proper conclusion.

TAFSIR OF QUR'AN THROUGH THE ARABIC LANGUAGE

The fifth source of tafsīr is the Arabic language itself. In several places throughout the Qur'ān, Allāh reminds the listener that He has revealed the Qur'ān in the Arabic language. Allāh says in Surah Yūsuf, "Indeed, We have sent it down as an Arabic Qur'ān that you might understand."[74] In Surah Al-Zumar, Allāh says, "[It is] an Arabic Qur'ān, without any deviance that they might become righteous."[75] Similarly, in Surah Fuṣilat Allāh says, "A Book whose verses have been detailed, an Arabic Qur'ān for a people who know."[76] Since the Qur'ān has been revealed in Arabic, the language itself is considered to be a source of interpretation.

In order to have a complete and accurate understanding of the Qur'ān, it is necessary for one to have a mastery of the language itself. It is impossible to properly understand the Qur'ān without knowledge of the language. As a

73 Bukhārī, *k. al-riqāq, b. mā yuhadharu min zaharah al-dunya wa al-tanāfusi fīha*, 6429

74 Qur'ān, 12:2

75 Qur'ān, 39:28

76 Qur'ān, 41:3

matter of fact, the scholars of the past were very severe in their attitudes towards those who attempted to interpret the Qur'ān without learning Arabic. For example, Imām Mālik ﷺ said, "If any person is brought to me, having interpreted the Qur'ān while he is ignorant of Arabic, I will make an example of him." Similarly, Mujāhid ﷺ said, "It is impermissible for any person who believes in Allāh and the last day to speak concerning the book of Allāh if he is not knowledgeable of the dialects of the Arabs."

A deep understanding of the language aids in understanding some of the difficult or rare words that are used in the Qur'ān. It also aids in understanding the usage and connotation of certain words. Sometimes the Qur'ān may use a certain expression or phrase that can only be understood through the usage of the language in the time that it was revealed.

TAFSIR OF QUR'AN THROUGH PERSONAL INTERPRETATION

The sixth source of tafsīr is through deliberation (ijtihād) and deduction (istinbāṭ) -- when a qualified scholar uses their own personal understanding or opinion to arrive at the meaning of a verse. Sometimes, there may not be a narration from the Prophet ﷺ or the Companions ﷺ regarding a particular verse. So a scholar may use their own understanding and opinion to come up with a plausible explanation.

When a commentator explains a verse using their own interpretation, it has to be based upon sound knowledge and conform to the general teachings of the Qur'ān and Sunnah. It cannot be based on a person's desires to make the Qur'ān conform to their personal perspectives or opinions regarding certain issues. A person has to have the proper prerequisites in order to do so.

This source of tafsīr is not an open license for people to interpret the Qur'ān according to their own flawed understandings or views. There are severe warnings against those who interpret the Qur'ān without proper knowledge. The Prophet ﷺ said, "Whoever says anything about the Qur'ān with his own personal opinion should prepare his seat in the Fire." In another narration the Prophet ﷺ said, "Whoever says anything about the Qur'ān with his own personal opinion, and is right, is still mistaken."

Imam al-Suyūṭī ﷺ mentions fifteen disciplines a person must master in order to be qualified to interpret the Qur'ān. They are:

1. knowledge of the Arabic language and its vocabulary
2. knowledge of Arabic grammar (naḥwu)
3. knowledge of Arabic morphology (ṣarf)
4. knowledge of Arabic words and word structure (ishtiqāq)
5. knowledge of Arabic rhetoric
6. eloquence
7. manners of oratory
8. knowledge of Qirā'āt
9. knowledge of the principles of fiqh (uṣūl al-fiqh)
10. knowledge of fiqh
11. knowledge of asbāb al-nuzūl
12. knowledge of nāsikh and mansūkh
13. knowledge of ḥadīth
14. knowledge of 'ulūm al-Qur'ān
15. divine endowment

Based on this criteria mentioned by Imām al-Suyūṭī, tafsīr is not a simple affair. It requires a great deal of expertise, skills, and knowledge. It requires an individual to invest a lot of time and energy in studying various subjects and disciplines. Commenting on the Qur'ān is a specialized art that should only be done by those who have the requisite qualifications to do so.

FAMOUS WORKS OF TAFSIR

Amongst the different branches of Islamic Studies tafsīr carries a unique and distinguished position. It is considered to be one of the most important and noble branches of knowledge because it aids in understanding the book of Allah ﷻ. In addition to being the most important and noble branch of study, it is perhaps also one of the most difficult to write about. Tafsīr is a discipline that requires a deep knowledge of all the other Islamic Sciences.

Because of its importance it has been given special attention throughout Islamic history. There have been several significant works of tafsīr produced in which the authors try their best to explain the meanings, lessons, wisdoms, reminders, rulings, beauty, language and eloquence of the Qur'ān. Oftentimes authors would focus their attention on one aspect. For example, some would focus on the linguistic aspect and others would focus on the legal aspect. Some would even address multiple aspects. Some works of tafsīr are extremely long filling up multiple volumes while others may be short and brief. There are hundreds if not thousands of works on tafsīr that can fill up an entire library. This chapter will introduce some of the most famous works of tafsīr, both classical and contemporary.

TAFSĪR IBN JARĪR

The full title of the work is *Jāmi' al-Bayān 'an Ta'wīl Āy Al-Qur'ān* (The Comprehensive Explanation of the Interpretation of the Verse of the Qur'ān). This is the monumental work of Abū Ja'far Muḥammad ibn Jarīr al-Ṭabari (310), simply known as al-Ṭabari, who was a well-known commentator, ḥadīth expert, jurist and historian. The commentary fills fifteen large volumes and was used as a primary source for later works of tafsīr. He comments on a verse by mentioning several narrations, sometimes up to a dozen, that explain the meanings of the verse. He then provides his reasoning for which meaning he feels is the strongest or most appropriate. He also discusses the different recitations of a verse and quotes lines of classical poetry to clarify the meanings of difficult words. Imām al-Suyūṭī ﷺ said regarding this work, "And his book is the best and greatest of all tafāsīr." Imām al-Nawawi ﷺ said, "The Ummah has agreed that nothing has ever rivaled the tafsīr of al-Ṭabari." Most scholars use it as a work of reference and research.

TAFSĪR IBN KATHĪR

This is perhaps the most famous, commonly read and studied tafsīr throughout the Muslim world. It is entitled *Tafsīr Al-Qur'ān Al-'Aẓīm* (The Explanation of the Great Qur'ān). It was written by the distinguished scholar of the eighth century, Ḥāfiẓ 'Imād al-Dīn Abū al-Fida Ismā'īl ibn Kathīr al-Dimishqi (774), simply known as ibn Kathīr. Tafsīr ibn Kathīr has been published multiple times in four large volumes. In his work he focused on narrations that explain the meanings, context and lessons of the verses. He explained the meanings in a way that is easy to read and understand.

TAFSĪR AL-QURṬUBI

The work is entitled *al-Jāmi' li Aḥkām al-Qur'ān* (The Compiler for the Rulings of the Qur'ān). It was written by the erudite scholar of Andalusia

Abū 'Abdillah Muḥammad ibn Aḥmad Abi Bakr ibn Faraḥ al-Qurṭubi (671), better known as Imām al-Qurṭubi. He was a well-known Māliki jurist and focused on the legal rulings that can be derived from the Qur'ān. While doing so he also explained the verses in detail highlighting the meanings of difficult words and explaining the eloquence and beauty of Allah's words. He also narrated a number of aḥādīth related to the verses. The work extends over twenty-four volumes and has been published several times.

TAFSĪR AL-RĀZI

The title of the work is *Mafātīḥ al-Ghayb* (Keys of the Unseen), but it is more popularly known as *al-Tafsīr al-Kabīr* (The Large Commentary). It was written by the well-known Imām Muḥammad ibn 'Umar al-Rāzi (606), better known as Fakhr al-Dīn al-Rāzi. He was an expert in theology, Arabic grammar and philosophy. In his work he discusses a number of rational and scholastic debates while refuting unorthodox sects of Islam. His work is considered to be a very unique contribution to the field of tafsīr. It fills eight large volumes and has been published several times.

AL-BAḤR AL-MUḤIṬ

The work is entitled *al-Baḥr al-Muḥiṭ* (The Encompassing Ocean). It was written by the distinguished scholar Abū Ḥayyān al-Gharnāṭi al-Andalūsi (754) who was an expert and master of Arabic grammar, syntax and rhetoric. Since he was an expert of the language his work is full of unique discussions on grammar, syntax and rhetoric. He placed a lot of emphasis on investigating and explaining the meanings of every word.

TAFSĪR AL-BAGHAWI

The title of the work is *Ma'ālim al-Tanzīl* (Milestones of Revelation). It was written by the well-known Shāf'ī jurist Abū Muḥammad Husayn ibn Masʿūd al-Baghawī (516). He was recognized as a scholar of tafsīr, ḥadīth and jurisprudence. It's a relatively short tafsīr expanding over four volumes that focuses on the vocabulary of the verses as well as explaining them through various narrations.

TAFSĪR AL-JALĀLAYN

One of the most widely-read and studied works of tafsīr across the Muslim world because of its simplicity and brevity. It was written by the two Jalāl's: Jalāl al-Dīn Muḥammad ibn Aḥmad al-Maḥalli (864) and his student the famous Jalāl al-Dīn al-Suyūṭī (911). Jalāl al-Dīn al-Maḥalli started the work from Surah al-Kahf and worked his way to the end of Surah al-Nās and then al-Fātiḥah. He passed away before completing the other half and the work was completed by his student Jalāl al-Dīn al-Suyūṭī. Both of these individuals were prolific scholars whose biographies can fill pages. Al-Suyūṭī is perhaps the most prolific author in Islamic history. Approximately seven-hundred works are attributed to him covering every discipline within Islamic Studies. This particular tafsīr is short, concise yet comprehensive and is often the first work of tafsīr studied by students of Islamic Studies. It is published in one volume and has been translated into English.

RŪḤ AL-MĀ'NĪ

The full name of this tafsīr is *Rūḥ al-Mā'ani fī Tafsīr al-Qur'ān al-'Aẓīm wa al-Sab' al-Mathāni* written by the Iraqi scholar Abū al-Thanā Shihāb al-Dīn Maḥmūd ibn 'Abdillah al-Ālūsi. This commentary is extremely expansive comprising of thirty volumes. He made his best possible effort to make the tafsīr comprehensive. There are exhaustive discussions on language, syntax, recitations, rhetoric, jurisprudence, creed, scholastics, philosophy, astronomy, mysticism, and related hadith. It is considered to be a very beneficial resource in understanding the many meanings of the Qur'ān.

IN THE SHADE OF THE QUR'ĀN

The Arabic title of this work is *Fī Ḍhilāl al-Qur'ān*. It was written by the Egyptian author, Islamic thinker, poet and leading member of the Muslim Brotherhood Syed Qutb (1966). It is a contemporary commentary on the Qur'ān and is very different from the scholastic works of tafsīr that focus on language. grammar, syntax, recitations and rulings. He wrote it over a period of fifteen years, most of which were spent in prison. In it he shared his personal thoughts and insights regarding the meanings of verses in the light of classical interpretations. He was a very eloquent writer and his eloquence is captured in the way this work flows seamlessly from one verse to the next. This work has been translated to English and is a unique and beneficial addition to the corpus of tafsīr literature.

MĀ'RIF AL-QUR'ĀN

This is the most famous work of the late Grand Mufti of Pakistan Muḥammad Shafī' al-'Uthmāni (1976), the father of the well-known jurist and scholar Mufti Taqi 'Uthmāni. Originally written in urdu, the author based this work off of the most famous classical works of tafsīr such as Tafsīr al-Ṭabari, ibn Kathīr, al-Qurṭubi, al-Rāzi, al-Baḥr al-Muḥiṭ and Rūḥ al-Mā'nī. He wrote the work in a very simple narrative style making it easily accessible for the average person to read. Not only does it include the discussions and analysis of the Qur'ān found in the classical works of tafsīr, it also tries to answer contemporary questions and issues in a logical and scholarly manner. It is used as a good reference book on Islamic topics and has been translated to English.

11

HOW TO APPROACH THE QUR'AN

One of the words used by Allāh ﷻ to describe the Qur'ān is *mubārak*, or blessed. This one-word description of the Qur'ān is actually very comprehensive. Every single aspect of the Qur'ān is blessed: its words, meanings, style, stories, commands, and prohibitions. Its recitation, memorization, interpretation, learning, and teaching are all acts of worship that bring huge amounts of rewards and blessings.

Part of its blessings is that those who learn it and teach it to others are considered to be the best of people. The Prophet ﷺ said, "The best amongst you are those who learn the Qur'ān and teach it."[77] For every single letter of the Qur'ān that is recited, a person is rewarded with a good deed that is multiplied by ten. "Whoever recites a letter from the book of Allāh, then for them is a good deed, and a good deed is multiplied by ten. I am not saying that *Alif lām mīm* is one letter, but *alif* is a letter, *lām* is a letter, and *mīm* is a letter."[78] The Qur'ān will intercede for its companion on the Day of Judgment. "Recite the Qur'ān because it will come as an intercessor for its companion on the Day of Judgment."[79] Through the Qur'ān, some nations are elevated while others are lowered.

There are several other narrations that mention the virtues, blessings,

77 Bukhārī, *k. fadā'il al-qur'ān, b. khayrukum man ta'llama al-qur'ān wa 'allamahu*, 5027

78 Tirmidhī, *k. fadā'il al-qur'ān 'an rasulillah*

79 Muslim, *k. salah al-musāfirīn, b. fadl qirā'ah al-qur'ān wa surah al-baqarah*, 804

and rewards for reciting the words of Allāh ﷻ. It is clear from these narrations that reading the Qur'ān is not like reading any other book. As a matter of fact, the Qur'ān is not like any other book. It does not follow the format of known genres of literature. It is not structured like a novel, text-book, or any other type of fictional or non-fictional writing. It has its own unique structure and format. The chapters, or Surahs, of the Qur'ān are not organized topically or chronologically. For example, all the verses dealing with justice are not gathered under one chapter. So before studying the Qur'ān, it is important to know how the Qur'ān is structured.

STRUCTURE OF THE QUR'AN

The Qur'ān consists of 114 surahs, which is usually translated as "chapters," starting with Surah al-Fātiḥah ("The Opening") and ending with Surah al-Nās (Mankind). Each surah is made up of a different number of āyāt, translated as "verses," the longest surah being 284 verses and the shortest just 4. Each of the āyāt are also of varying lengths, the shortest being two words and the longest being more than a hundred. There are a total of 6,235 āyāt in the Qur'ān.[80] As a general rule, the longer surahs appear at the beginning of the Qur'ān and the surahs gradually become shorter as the text proceeds.

Each surah has a specific name (sometimes, even several names). Each surah is separated by the *basmalah (bismillahi al-rahmān al-rahīm)* with the exception of surah al-Tawbah. The order of the āyāt in each surah as well as the sequence of the surahs was determined by the Prophet ﷺ through divine revelation.

In addition to being divided into surahs (chapters) and āyāt (verses), the Qur'ān is divided almost equally into thirty parts called ajzā' (s. juz). This division is not based on subject matter or meaning but is done so that Muslims can easily manage reciting the entire Qur'ān at least once a month, especially in the month of Ramadān. Each juz is further divided into two halves, in Arabic, *hizb*, which are also divided into halves and quarters. Again, these divisions were made later on to give a common reader a certain structure to follow for recitation as well as memorization.

Another common division in several copies of the Qur'ān is that of a

80 There are a few different opinions regarding the number of āyāt in the Qur'ān because of a difference in numbering some of the verses.

rukūʿ, or section. This division is marked on the margins of the page with the letter ع. The purpose of this division is to mark the amount of a sūrah that can be read in one unit of prayer. These divisions are usually done according to the meanings and subject matter.

STUDYING THE QUR'AN

As mentioned above, reciting the Qurʾān is an extremely virtuous act that carries a lot of reward and blessings. Recitation of the Qurʾān is an integral part of a Muslim's daily life. The first step in studying the Qurʾān should be learning how to recite it properly in the Arabic Language under the tutelage of a skilled reciter. A person should learn how to recite the Qurʾān with tajwīd[81] and become as proficient and fluent as possible in recitation. As the Prophet ﷺ encouraged us, "The one who recites the Qur'an and he is proficient in it, then he is with the noble and blessed Angels, and the one who recites it and it is difficult for him, then he gets two rewards."[82] After learning how to recite the Qurʾān properly one should have a set amount that is recited every single day.

However, as mentioned before, the main purpose of reciting the Qurʾān is to think, ponder, and reflect over its meanings and to bring its teachings into one's daily practical life. One of the best ways to do so is by reading a translation along with a commentary of the portion of the Qurʾān that's being recited daily. There are a number of different English translations to choose from. A translation that is highly recommended by a number of scholars is *The Qur'an* by M.A.S. Abdel Haleem. A few highly recommended commentaries that have been translated to English are *Tafsīr ibn Kathīr*, *Mā'riful Qur'ān*, and *In the Shade of the Qur'ān*. In addition to that there are several beneficial lectures covering the explanation of certain chapters of the Qur'ān found online.

The Qur'ān is first and foremost a book of guidance. It contains guidance for every single aspect of human life. It contains a detailed explanation of what humanity needs in terms of guidance, success both in this life and the next and salvation. Allah ﷻ says, "This revelation is no fabrication: it is

81 Tajwīd refers to the set of rules that teaches one how pronounce every letter of the Qurʾān from its proper point of articulation (makhraj) along with its attributes (Sifāt).

82 Tirmidhī, k. fadā'il al-qur'ān 'an rasulillah

a confirmation of the truth of what was sent before it; an explanation of everything; a guide and a blessing for those who believe."[83] It should be treated as a personal guidebook: a roadmap towards faith, practice, morality, ethics, God-consciousness, obedience, worship, paradise and essentially the Divine. One should take the time to read, reflect and ponder over the meanings of the verses and then internalize their message through practice. "We have made it easy to learn lessons from the Qur'ān: will anyone take heed?"[84]

83 Qur'ān, 12:111
84 Qur'ān, 54:17

FURTHER READING

ENGLISH WORKS

- Qadhi, Yasir. *An Introduction to the Sciences of the Qur'aan*. Birmingham, UK: Al-Hidaayah, 1999
- Usmani, Muḥammad Taqi. *An Approach to the Qurānic Sciences*. Karachi, Pakistan: Darul Isha'at, 2000
- Von Denffer, Ahmad. *Ulum Al-Qurān: An Introduction to the Sciences of the Qurān*. USA: The Islamic Foundation, 2009

ARABIC WORKS

- Al-Suyūṭī, Jalāl al-Dīn. *Al-Itqān fī 'ulūm al-Qur'ān*. Beirut: Al-Maktabah Al- 'Asriyyah, 2006
- Al-Sābūnī, Muḥammad 'Ali. *Al-Tibyān fī 'ulūm al-Qur'ān*. Karachi: Maktabah Al-Bushra, 2010

BIBLIOGRAPHY

- Al-Bukhārī, Muḥammad b. Ismā'īl. *Al-Jāmi' Al-Ṣaḥīḥ*. Cited by chapter, subchapter system.
- b. Al-Ḥajjāj, Muslim. *Ṣaḥīḥ Muslim*. Cited by chapter, subchapter system.
- Al-Nasā'ī, Ahmad b. Shu'ayb. *Sunan*. Cited by chapter, subchapter system.
- Al-Sijistāni, Abū Dāwūd. *Al-Sunan*. Cited by chapter, subchapter system.
- Al-Tirmidhī, Muḥammad b. 'Īsā. *Al-Jāmi'*. Cited by chapter, subchapter system.
- Al-Suyūṭī, Jalāl al-Dīn. *Al-Itqān fī 'ulūm al-Qur'ān*. Beirut: Al-Maktabah Al- 'Asriyyah, 2006
- Al-Hakim, Muḥammad b. 'Abdallah al-Naysāburi. *Al-Mustadrak 'ala al-Ṣaḥiḥayn*.
- Usmani, Muḥammad Taqi. *An Approach to the Qurānic Sciences*. Karachi, Pakistan: Darul Isha'at, 2000
- Al-Suyūṭī, Jalāl al-Dīn. *Al-Itqān fī 'ulūm al-Qur'ān*. Beirut: Al-Maktabah Al- 'Asriyyah, 2006

ABOUT THE AUTHOR

Shaykh Furhan Zubairi was born in 1983 in Indianapolis, IN. Shortly thereafter, he moved and spent most of his youth in Southern California, graduating from high school in Irvine in 2001. He began his pursuit of Islamic knowledge and spirituality at the Institute of Knowledge (IOK) in 1998 where he started the memorization of the Quran and studied the primary books in the Islamic sciences and Arabic language. After starting college, he took a break and went to Karachi, Pakistan for 9 months to complete the memorization of the Quran at Jami'ah Binoria. He returned home and completed his B.S. in Biological Sciences from the University of California, Irvine in 2005. He then traveled to Egypt to further his studies of the Arabic language. Thereafter, his pursuit of Islamic knowledge led him back to Pakistan where he completed a formal 'Alamiyyah degree (Masters in Arabic and Islamic Studies) at the famous Jami'ah Darul-Uloom in Karachi, where he studied with prominent scholars. He has obtained numerous ijaazaat (traditional licenses) in the six authentic books of hadith Siha Sittah as well as the Muwattas of Imam Malik and Imam Muhammad and has also received certification in the field of Islamic Finance. Shaykh Furhan Zubairi serves as the Director of Religious Education and is the Dean of the full-time Seminary program (IOKseminary.com) at the Institute of Knowledge in Diamond Bar, CA. He regularly delivers khutbahs and lectures at various Islamic Centers and events in Southern California.

The Institute of Knowledge Curriculum Series is a collection of books designed to build literacy amongst the Muslim community in the major branches of Islamic Studies including ʿAqīdah, Qur'ān, Ḥadīth, Fiqh, Uṣūl al-Fiqh, Sīrah and Tazkiyyah. The books go hand in hand with the courses offered through the IOK Extension Program, which provides educational courses, programs and seminars that extend the Institute's resources to the wider local and international community.

FORTHCOMING WORKS:

- A Brief Introduction to ʿUlūm al-Ḥadīth
- A Brief Introduction to Uṣūl al-Fiqh
- A Brief Introduction to Tajwīd
- A Brief Commentary on Imām Nawawi's Forty Ḥadīth
- Tafsīr of Juz ʿAmma

NOTES

NOTES

NOTES

NOTES

NOTES

NOTES

Made in the USA
Las Vegas, NV
29 August 2024

94554317R00062